Kaplan Publishing are constantly finding new ways to make a difference to your studies and our exciting online resources really do offer something different to students looking for exam success.

This book comes with free MyKaplan online resources so that you can study anytime, anywhere

Having purchased this book, you have access to the following online study materials:

CONTENT	ACCA (including FFA,FAB,FMA)		AAT		FIA (excluding FFA,FAB,FMA)	
	Text	Kit	Text	Kit	Text	Kit
iPaper version of the book	✓	✓	✓	✓	✓	✓
Interactive electronic version of the book	✓					
Progress tests with instant answers	✓		✓			
Mock assessments online			✓	✓		
Material updates	✓	✓	✓	✓	✓	✓
Latest official ACCA exam questions		✓				
Extra question assistance using the signpost icon*		✓				
Timed questions with an online tutor debrief using the clock icon*		✓				
Interim assessment including questions and answers	✓				✓	
Technical articles	✓	✓			✓	✓

* Excludes F1, F2, F3, FFA, FAB, FMA

How to access your online resources

Kaplan Financial students will already have a MyKaplan account and these extra resources will be available to you online. You do not need to register again, as this process was completed when you enrolled. If you are having problems accessing online materials, please ask your course administrator.

If you are already a registered MyKaplan user go to www.MyKaplan.co.uk and log in. Select the 'add a book' feature and enter the ISBN number of this book and the unique pass key at the bottom of this card. Then click 'finished' or 'add another book'. You may add as many books as you have purchased from this screen.

If you purchased through Kaplan Flexible Learning or via the Kaplan Publishing website you will automatically receive an e-mail invitation to MyKaplan. Please register your details using this email to gain access to your content. If you do not receive the e-mail or book content, please contact Kaplan Flexible Learning.

If you are a new MyKaplan user register at www.MyKaplan.co.uk and click on the link contained in the email we sent you to activate your account. Then select the 'add a book' feature, enter the ISBN number of this book and the unique pass key at the bottom of this card. Then click 'finished' or 'add another book'.

Your Code and Information

This code can only be used once for the registration of one book online. This registration and your online content will expire when the final sittings for the examinations covered by this book taken place. Please allow one hour from the time you submit your book details for us to pro your request.

Please scratch the film to access your MyKaplan code.

Please be aware that this code is case-sensitive and you will need to include the dashes within the passcode, but not when entering the ISBN. For further technical support, please visit www.MyKaplan.co.uk

BASIC COSTING

Qualifications and Credit Framework

AQ2013 Level 2 Certificate in Accounting

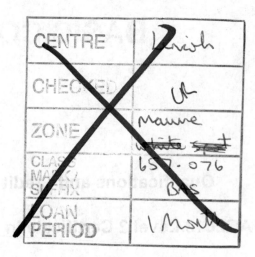

British Library Cataloguing-in-Publication Data

A catalogue record for this book is available from the British Library.

Published by
Kaplan Publishing UK
Unit 2, The Business Centre
Molly Millars Lane
Wokingham
Berkshire
RG41 2QZ

ISBN 978 0 85732 871 7

We are grateful to the Association of Accounting Technicians for permission to reproduce past assessment materials and example tasks based on the new syllabus. The solutions to past answers and similar activities in the style of the new syllabus have been prepared by Kaplan Publishing.

3001888
£ 18.00

CONTENTS

Introduction   v

Unit guide   vii

The assessment   xv

Study skills   xvii

Terminology   xxi

STUDY TEXT AND WORKBOOK

Chapter		Study text	Workbook Activities Answers
1	Cost classification	1	131
2	Coding of costs and income	23	133
3	Materials and inventory	39	135
4	Labour costs	71	138
5	Budgeting	87	139
6	Spreadsheets	103	140
Mock Assessment Questions			145
Mock Assessment Answers			161
Index			I.1

INTRODUCTION

HOW TO USE THESE MATERIALS

These Kaplan Publishing learning materials have been carefully designed to make your learning experience as easy as possible and to give you the best chance of success in your AAT assessments.

They contain a number of features to help you in the study process.

The sections on the Unit Guide, the Assessment and Study Skills should be read before you commence your studies.

They are designed to familiarise you with the nature and content of the assessment and to give you tips on how best to approach your studies.

STUDY TEXT

This study text has been specially prepared for the revised AAT qualification introduced in September 2013.

It is written in a practical and interactive style:

- key terms and concepts are clearly defined

- all topics are illustrated with practical examples with clearly worked solutions based on sample tasks provided by the AAT in the new examining style

- frequent practice activities throughout the chapters ensure that what you have learnt is regularly reinforced

- 'pitfalls' and 'examination tips' help you avoid commonly made mistakes and help you focus on what is required to perform well in your examination

- practice workbook activities can be completed at the end of each chapter.

WORKBOOK

The workbook comprises:

Practice activities at the end of each chapter with solutions at the end of the text, to reinforce the work covered in each chapter.

The questions are divided into their relevant chapters and students may either attempt these questions as they work through the textbook, or leave some or all of these until they have completed the textbook as a final revision of what they have studied.

ICONS

The study chapters include the following icons throughout.

They are designed to assist you in your studies by identifying key definitions and the points at which you can test yourself on the knowledge gained.

 Definition

These sections explain important areas of Knowledge which must be understood and reproduced in an assessment.

 Example

The illustrative examples can be used to help develop an understanding of topics before attempting the activity exercises.

 Activity

These are exercises which give the opportunity to assess your understanding of all the assessment areas.

UNIT GUIDE

Purpose of the unit

The purpose of the Basic Costing unit is to give students a basic introduction to costing at level 2, recognising the need to build a sound foundation in costing to give the candidate the relevant knowledge and skills to take forward to the more complex costing and accounting units they will study at levels 3 and 4. At the same time students are made aware of the importance of the costing system as a source of information for internal management decision making as contrasted against financial accounting which looks outwards. Students need to understand what constitutes costs in different organisations. For instance a cost structure within a manufacturing industry will be different from a cost structure within a service industry and as a consequence the costing systems will differ.

Another learning outcome recognises the importance of spreadsheets as a means of communicating costing information. The assessment will test students' understanding of spreadsheets as a method of conveying costing information, the important phrase here being conveying costing information. It must be stressed that students are not being assessed on their spreadsheet ability, but on their basic understanding of spreadsheets as a method of presenting costing information. The assessment will be a mixture of simulation to test skill, and knowledge based tasks to test understanding. It will be assumed that students will have had exposure to spreadsheets as a method of presenting information in preparation for this assessment.

Learning objectives

The Basic Costing unit requires students to have an underlying knowledge and understanding of the nature of a cost accounting system within an organisation and its component parts as well as an understanding of how it operates. Students will also be required to demonstrate the skills they have acquired in using the cost system to record or extract data and providing information on actual and expected costs using a simulated spreadsheet format.

It should be stressed that the unit provides an introduction to costing and are looking to develop basic skills that the candidate will build upon in later studies.

On completion of these units the learner will be able to:

- Understand the nature of inventory at its different stages in the production process; learners will be expected to be familiar with the components of a manufacturing account.

- Identify the characteristics of FIFO, LIFO and AVCO as methods of inventory valuation and cost an issue and value closing inventory by each method.

- Classify costs by nature, element, behaviour and function.

- Identify the characteristics of time rate and piecework as methods of labour remuneration, along with calculations of overtime and bonuses.

- Identify differences between Cost, Profit and Investment centres.

- Explain and use different methods of coding data.

- Understand what a variance is and calculate a variance by comparing actual cost with budgeted cost.

- Identify whether a variance is adverse or favourable.

- Identify whether a variance is significant and the manager to whom this should be reported.

- Use spreadsheets to provide information on actual and budget income and expenditure.

Learning Outcomes and Assessment criteria

Each unit consists of three learning outcomes, each comprising of a number of assessment criteria.

The learning outcomes are:

1   Understand the cost recording system within an organisation.

2   Be able to use the cost recording system to record or extract data.

3   Be able to use spreadsheets to provide information on actual and budgeted income and expenditure.

Knowledge

To perform this unit effectively you will need to know and understand the following:

		Chapter
1	**Understand the cost recording system within an organisation.**	
1.1	Explain the nature of an organisation's business transactions in relation to its accounting systems.	1
1.2	Explain the purpose and structure of a costing system within an organisation.	1
1.3	Identify the relationships between the costing and accounting systems within the organisation.	1
1.4	Identify sources of income and expenditure information for historic, current and forecast periods.	All
1.5	Identify types of cost, profit and investment centres.	1
2	**Be able to use the cost recording system to record or extract data.**	
2.1	Explain how materials, labour and expenses are classified and recorded.	2, 3, 4
2.2	Explain different methods of coding data.	2
2.4	Classify different types of inventory as: raw materials, part-finished goods (work-in-progress), finished goods.	3
2.7	Explain the nature of expenses and distinguish between fixed, variable and semi-variable overheads.	1
3	**Be able to use spreadsheets to provide information on actual and budgeted income and expenditure.**	
3.2	Explain how spreadsheets can be used to present information on income and expenditure and to facilitate internal reporting.	6

Skills

To perform this unit effectively you will need to be able to do the following:

Chapter

2   Be able to use the cost recording system to record or extract data.

2.3 Classify and code cost information for materials, labour and expenses.   1, 2

2.5 Calculate inventory valuations and issues of inventory using these methods: First in first out (FIFO), Last in first out (LIFO), Weighted average (AVCO).   3

2.6 Use these methods to calculate payments for labour: time-rate, piecework rate, bonuses.   4

2.8 Calculate the direct cost of a product or service.   1, 2

3   Be able to use spreadsheets to provide information on actual and budgeted income and expenditure.

3.1 Enter income and expenditure data into a spreadsheet.   6

3.3 Enter budgeted and actual data on income and expenditure into a spreadsheet to make a comparison of the results and identify differences.   5, 6

3.4 Use basic spreadsheet functions and guidance.   6

3.5 Format the spreadsheet to present data in a clear and unambiguous manner and in accordance with organisational requirements.   6

Delivery guidance

The AAT have provided delivery guidance giving further details of the way in which the unit will be assessed.

Delivery Guidance: Basic Costing

1 Understand the cost recording system within an organisation

1.1 Explain the nature of the organisation's business transactions in relation to its accounting systems.

Students need to understand what constitutes cost in different organisations. For instance a cost structure within a manufacturing industry will be different from a cost structure within a service industry and as a consequence the costing systems will differ. Students will be required to identify the elements of cost (materials, labour, and overheads) within an organisation and the nature of the cost (direct or indirect), which will be assessed by two tasks in the assessment.

1.2 Explain the purpose and structure of a costing system within an organisation.

Students must develop an understanding of what a costing system brings to an organisation. In order to do this they must be able to classify cost by element, nature and behaviour (fixed, variable or semi-variable). From this students must be able to explain the purpose and role of the costing system in particular determining product cost and hence selling price, valuing inventory, providing information for financial statements and management decision making. The assessment for this criteria will be through one task testing understanding of a costing system and what it brings to an organisation.

1.3 Identify the relationships between the costing and accounting systems within the organisation.

Students must understand the nature of the costing and accounting systems within the organisation. This requires knowledge of their purpose and what they are trying to achieve. Essential to this is the need to understand how each system uses cost; the costing system dependent upon the information that is required for it (product cost will need cost classified by element) contrasted with the accounting system which will require cost classified by function (production, administration, selling and distribution etc). Assessment testing differences between costing and accounting systems will be explicit to one task and the use of cost will be explicit to two tasks.

1.4 Identify sources of income and expenditure information for historic, current and forecast periods.

Students must be able to identify how financial accounts are used to provide data for historic periods, how actual or estimated materials and labour costs and estimated overheads are used, for instance, to arrive at a job cost for the current period, and how standard and budgeted costs are used for forecast periods. This criteria will be implicitly assessed over a number of tasks throughout the assessment.

1.5 Identify types of cost, profit and investment centres.

Students will be expected to identify what is meant by a cost centre, a profit centre and an investment centre, why they are used in a costing system and be able to classify a given centre appropriately. Such knowledge will be assessed explicitly through the two coding tasks and implicitly in tasks relating to learning outcome 3.

2 Be able to use the cost recording system to record or extract data

2.1 Explain how materials, labour and expenses are classified and recorded.

Students must be able to classify and record across a range of business organisations materials, labour and expenses as either direct or indirect; fixed or variable. Assessment will be across a range of tasks covering the elements of cost, materials, labour and expenses/overheads. (Note that, for this unit, expenses are interpreted as overheads and throughout the guidance and ensuing assessments the terms expenses and overheads are interchangeable. It is acknowledged there is a category of expense termed 'direct expenses', however such a classification is beyond the scope of this unit. For assessment purposes, expenses will be known as overheads and will always be indirect in nature.)

2.2 Explain different methods of coding data.

Students must be able to explain and understand a range of coding systems (numeric, alphabetic, alpha-numeric). Students' understanding will be assessed through two coding tasks in the assessments.

2.3 Classify and code cost information for materials, labour and expenses.

Students will be assessed on their ability to code materials, labour and expenses/overheads using numeric and alpha numeric systems of coding over two tasks.

2.4 Classify different types of inventory as: raw materials, part-finished goods (work-in-progress), finished goods.

Students must understand the flow of inventory through the stages of manufacture and be able to identify the components of a cost statement for manufactured goods appreciating the classification of inventory in arriving at direct materials used, direct cost, factory cost of goods manufactured and cost of goods sold. Students will be required to calculate sub-totals and the total of the cost statement.

2.5 Calculate inventory valuations and issues of inventories using these methods: First in first out (FIFO), Last in first out (LIFO), Weighted average (AVCO).

Students must be able to use FIFO, LIFO and Weighted average (AVCO) as methods of costing issues of inventories from stores and valuing closing inventories. Assessment will be over two tasks. The first will require students to determine the method from the data given and the second will require students to calculate the cost of one issue and value of closing inventory for each method.

2.6 Use these methods to calculate payments for labour: time-rate, piecework rate, bonuses.

Students will be required to understand the methods of payment for labour in order to calculate payments. Note that time-rate will include calculation of an overtime time-rate. Assessments will be over three tasks that will test ability to identify a payment method and calculate pay using each method. Students will not be required to have knowledge of specific bonus schemes.

2.7 Explain the nature of expenses and distinguish between fixed, variable and semi-variable overheads.

Students will be expected to define what expenses/overheads are and then classify their behaviour as fixed, variable or semi-variable. A cost behaviour task will also require students to demonstrate their understanding by showing how costs including overheads behave with changes in the level of output.

2.8 Calculate the direct cost of a product or service.

Students will be assessed over two tasks. Although a new assessment criteria, this was assessed implicitly before. For future assessments students will be expected to identify direct (prime) cost in a manufacturing account in one task and build up a product cost with the identification of direct cost and total cost.

3   Be able to use spreadsheets to provide information on actual and budgeted income and expenditure

3.1   Enter income and expenditure data into a spreadsheet.

The task for this assessment criteria could be a range of product costs or a range of outputs. The data will be set out in a simulated spreadsheet. Students will be expected to format the spreadsheet by completing headers and will also be expected to demonstrate their costing skills by completing the table data. As supplementary students will be expected to identify or state formulas for totals and other calculations.

3.2   Explain how spreadsheets can be used to present information on income and expenditure and to facilitate internal reporting.

Students will be expected to demonstrate their understanding of how spreadsheets can be used to present information through knowledge based tasks that will require students to select the correct statement or recognise it as being true or false.

3.3   Enter budgeted and actual data on income and expenditure into a spreadsheet to provide a comparison of the results and identify differences.

Students will be expected to understand basic budgeting and the concepts budgeted costs, actual cost, budgeted income, actual income and budgeted profit. Students will also be expected to understand the basic variances arising from the above comparisons and recognise them as being either favourable or adverse. It must be stressed that the analysis will be at a basic level and no understanding of sub-variances will be required. Students will be presented with a simulated spreadsheet and they will be expected to complete heading and complete data entry using their costing skills to do so. Students will be expected to identify or state formulas for totals and other calculations.

3.4   Use basic spreadsheet functions and formulas.

Students will be expected to complete headings and totals for two simulated spreadsheets and will be expected to add, subtract, multiply, divide and total and recognise formulas for such. A separate task will see students presented with a set of budgeted data and variances and they could be asked to reorder, average or express as %.

3.5   Format the spreadsheet to present data in a clear and unambiguous manner and in accordance with organisational requirements.

Students will be expected to format a spreadsheet by reorganising data using functions such as ascending, descending, auto sum, etc. They will be expected to present significant variances in a clear and unambiguous manner to managers.

THE ASSESSMENT

The format of the assessment

The assessment will be in one section.

Expect to see 17 independent tasks. Several of these tasks will be broken down into more than one requirement.

Learners will be assessed by computer based assessment (CBA) and will be required to demonstrate competence across the entire assessment.

For the purpose of assessment the competency level for AAT assessment is set at 70 per cent.

Time allowed

The time allowed for this assessment is **120 minutes.**

STUDY SKILLS

Preparing to study

Devise a study plan

Determine which times of the week you will study.

Split these times into sessions of at least one hour for study of new material. Any shorter periods could be used for revision or practice.

Put the times you plan to study onto a study plan for the weeks from now until the assessment and set yourself targets for each period of study – in your sessions make sure you cover the whole course, activities and the associated questions in the workbook at the back of the manual.

If you are studying more than one unit at a time, try to vary your subjects as this can help to keep you interested and see subjects as part of wider knowledge.

When working through your course, compare your progress with your plan and, if necessary, re-plan your work (perhaps including extra sessions) or, if you are ahead, do some extra revision/practice questions.

Effective studying

Active reading

You are not expected to learn the text by rote, rather, you must understand what you are reading and be able to use it to pass the assessment and develop good practice.

A good technique is to use SQ3Rs – Survey, Question, Read, Recall, Review:

1   Survey the chapter

Look at the headings and read the introduction, knowledge, skills and content, so as to get an overview of what the chapter deals with.

2   Question

Whilst undertaking the survey, ask yourself the questions you hope the chapter will answer for you.

3   Read

Read through the chapter thoroughly working through the activities and, at the end, making sure that you can meet the learning objectives highlighted on the first page.

4   Recall

At the end of each section and at the end of the chapter, try to recall the main ideas of the section/chapter without referring to the text. This is best done after short break of a couple of minutes after the reading stage.

5   Review

Check that your recall notes are correct.

You may also find it helpful to re-read the chapter to try and see the topic(s) it deals with as a whole.

Note taking

Taking notes is a useful way of learning, but do not simply copy out the text. The notes must:

- be in your own words
- be concise
- cover the key points
- well organised
- be modified as you study further chapters in this text or in related ones.

Trying to summarise a chapter without referring to the text can be a useful way of determining which areas you know and which you don't.

Three ways of taking notes

1   Summarise the key points of a chapter

2   Make linear notes

A list of headings, subdivided with sub-headings listing the key points.

If you use linear notes, you can use different colours to highlight key points and keep topic areas together.

Use plenty of space to make your notes easy to use.

3 Try a diagrammatic form

The most common of which is a mind map.

To make a mind map, put the main heading in the centre of the paper and put a circle around it.

Draw lines radiating from this to the main sub-headings which again have circles around them.

Continue the process from the sub-headings to sub-sub-headings.

Highlighting and underlining

You may find it useful to underline or highlight key points in your study text – but do be selective.

You may also wish to make notes in the margins.

Revision phase

Kaplan has produced material specifically designed for your final examination preparation for this unit.

These include pocket revision notes and a bank of revision questions specifically in the style of the new syllabus.

Further guidance on how to approach the final stage of your studies is given in these materials.

Further reading

In addition to this text, you should also read the "Student section" of the "Accounting Technician" magazine every month to keep abreast of any guidance from the examiners.

Terminology

There are different terms used to mean the same thing – you will need to be aware of both sets of terminology.

UK GAAP	IAS
Profit and loss	Statement of profit or loss
Sales	Revenue
Balance sheet	Statement of financial position
Fixed assets	Non-current assets
Tangible assets	Property, plant and equipment
Stock	Inventory
Trade debtors	Trade receivables
Trade creditors	Trade payables
Capital	Equity
Profit	Retained earnings

Cost classification

1

Introduction

This chapter introduces the concepts of financial and management accounting, the terminology of cost, profit and investment centres and looks in detail at different ways of classifying costs.

KNOWLEDGE

1.1 Explain the nature of an organisation's business transactions in relation to its accounting systems.

1.2 Explain the purpose and structure of a costing system within an organisation.

1.3 Identify the relationships between the costing and accounting systems within the organisation.

1.5 Identify types of cost, profit and investment centres.

2.1 Explain how materials, labour and expenses are classified and recorded.

2.7 Explain the nature of expenses and distinguish between fixed, variable and semi-variable overheads.

SKILLS

2.8 Calculate the direct cost of a product or service.

CONTENTS

1 Financial accounting and management accounting
2 Terminology – cost units and cost centres
3 Cost classification

1 Financial accounting and management accounting

1.1 Introduction

Most businesses, whether large or small, generate large numbers of different types of transaction. To make sense of those transactions, they need to be recorded, summarised and analysed. In all businesses, it is the accounts department that performs these tasks.

From the raw data of the business's transactions, accountants provide **information for a wide range of interested parties**. Each party requires, however, slightly different information, dependent upon their interest in the business.

1.2 Financial accounting

Financial accounting provides information to **external groups**, such as the owners of the business, potential investors and HM Revenue and Customs (who uses this information to check that the business is paying the correct amount of tax).

Financial accounting could be described in simple terms as **keeping score**. The financial accounts produced are a **historic record** of transactions and are presented in a standard format laid down in law. These normally include:

- A statement of financial position (also known as a balance sheet)
- A statement of profit or loss (also known as an 'income statement' or 'profit and loss account').

Such statements are normally only produced **once or twice a year**.

Financial accounting is not, however, the only type of accounting. The other main type is Management accounting.

1.3 Management accounting

Management accounting provides information for **internal users**, such as the managers of the business.

Management accounting compares **actual results with predicted results** and tries to use information to make further predictions about the future.

It also provides information which managers can use to make **decisions**.

Management accounts can be produced in any format that is useful to the business and tend to be produced frequently, for instance every month.

1.4 The aims of management accounting

The aim of management accounting is to assist management in the following areas of running a business.

- **Planning**

  For example, through the preparation of annual budgets. This is a key aspect of management accounting.

- **Co-ordinating**

  Planning enables all departments to be co-ordinated and to work together.

- **Controlling**

  The comparison of actual results with the budget helps to identify areas where operations are not running according to plan.

  Investigating the causes, and acting on the results of that investigation, helps to control the activities of the business.

- **Communicating**

  Preparing budgets that are distributed to department managers helps to communicate the aims of the business to those managers.

- **Motivating**

  Management accounts include targets. These should motivate managers (and staff) and improve their performance.

  If the target is too difficult, however, it is likely to demotivate and it is unlikely to be achieved.

1.5 Useful management information

For **management information** to be of use to a particular group of managers, it must have the following attributes:

- **Relevant to their responsibilities**. For example, a production manager will want information about inventories, production levels, production performance, etc within his particular department.

- **Relevant to particular decisions**. For example, if deciding whether to close a division, managers would need to know the likely costs including lost sales, likely redundancies and so on.

- **Timely**. Information has to be up-to-date to be of any value.

- **Value**. The benefits of having the information must outweigh the cost of producing it.

1.6 Cost accounting

Cost accounting is part of management accounting. As its name suggests, it is concerned with **establishing costs**. It developed within manufacturing businesses where costs are most difficult to isolate and analyse.

Cost accounting is primarily directed at enabling management to perform the functions of **planning, control** and **decision making:**

(a) determining costs and profits during a control period

(b) valuing inventories of raw materials, work in progress and finished goods, and controlling inventory levels

(c) preparing budgets, forecasts and other control data for a forthcoming control period

(d) creating a reporting system which enables managers to take corrective action where necessary to control costs

(e) providing information for decision-making such as setting the selling price of products or services.

Items (a) and (b) are traditional **cost accounting roles**; (c) to (e) extend into management accounting.

 Activity 1

The table below lists some of the characteristics of financial accounting and management accounting systems.

Indicate the characteristics for each system by putting a tick in the relevant column of the table.

Characteristic	Financial accounting	Management accounting
Content can include anything useful.		
To help managers run the business.		
Formats dictated by accounting rules.		
Looks mainly at historical information.		
Produced for shareholders.		

2 Terminology – cost units and cost centres

2.1 Cost units

To help with the above purposes of planning, control and decision making, businesses often need to calculate a cost per unit of output.

A key question, however, is what exactly we mean by a "unit of output", or "**cost unit**". This will mean different things to different businesses but we always looks at what the business produces.

- A car manufacturer will want to determine the cost of each car and probably different components as well.

- In a printing firm, the cost unit could be the specific customer order.

- For a paint manufacturer, the unit could be a litre of paint.

- An accountancy firm will want to know the costs incurred for each client. To help with this it is common to calculate the cost per hour of chargeable time spent by staff.

- A hospital might wish to calculate the cost per patient treated, the cost of providing a bed for each day or the cost of an operation.

2.2 Cost centres

A **cost centre** is a small part of a business for which costs are determined. This varies from business to business but could include any of the following:

- The Research and Development department

- The Human Resources function

- A warehouse

- A factory in a particular location.

It is important to recognise that cost centre costs are necessary for control purposes, as well as for relating costs to cost units. This is because the manager of a cost centre will be responsible for the costs incurred.

 Activity 2

Suggest **ONE** suitable cost unit and **TWO** cost centres for a college of Further Education.

2.3 Cost, profit and investment centres

Some businesses use the term "cost centre" in a more precise way than that given above:

- A **cost centre** is when the manager of the centre (department or division or location or...) is responsible for costs but not revenue or investment. This is usually because the centre has no revenue stream.

  For example, a Research and Development department.

- A **profit centre** is when the manager of the centre (department or division or location or...) is responsible for costs and revenues but not investment.

  For example, a local supermarket where investment decisions are made by the main Board.

- An **investment centre** is when the manager of the centre (usually a division) is responsible for costs and revenues **and** the level of investment in the division.

  For example, the US subsidiary of a global firm. The CEO would usually have authority to open new factories, close others and so on.

3 Cost classification

3.1 Types of cost classification

Costs can be **classified** (collected into logical groups) in many ways. The particular classification selected will depend upon the purpose for which the resulting analysed data will be used, for example:

Purpose	Classification
Financial accounts	By function – cost of sales, distribution costs, administrative expenses.
Cost control	By element – materials, labour, other expenses.
Cost accounts	By relationship to cost units – direct, indirect.
Budgeting, decision making	By behaviour – fixed, variable.

3.2 Cost classification by function

For financial accounting purposes costs are split into the following categories:

- **Cost of sales** – also known as production costs. This category could include production labour, materials, supervisor salaries and factory rent.

- **Distribution costs** – this includes selling and distribution costs such as sales team commission and delivery costs.

- **Administrative costs** – this includes head office costs, IT support, HR support and so on.

- **Finance** – this refers to money paid to providers of finance (for example banks) and includes bank charges and interest charged on loans.

Note that one cost you will meet in the exam is depreciation. This is a measure of how much an asset is wearing out or being used up. The classification will depend on which asset is being depreciated. For example,

- Cost of sales – depreciation on a machine in the production line.

- Distribution – depreciation of a delivery van.

- Admin – depreciation of a computer in the accounts department.

 Activity 3

James plc makes mobile phones. Classify the following costs by function in the table below.

Cost	Production	Admin	Distribution
Purchases of plastic to make phone cases.			
IT director's bonus.			
Depreciation of factory building.			
Salaries of production workers.			
Insurance of sales team laptops.			

3.3 Cost classification by element

The simplest classification you will meet in the exam is splitting costs according to element as follows:

- **Materials** – includes raw materials for a manufacturer or alternatively the cost of goods that are to be resold in a retail organisation.

- **Labour** – Labour costs can consist of not only basic pay but overtime, commissions and bonuses as well.

- **Overheads** – this may also be referred to as **other expenses** and includes electricity, depreciation, rent and so on.

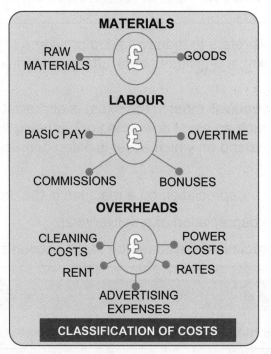

Activity 4

Classify the following costs for a supermarket chain by element in the table below.

Cost	Materials	Labour	Overheads
Tins of baked beans.			
Lighting costs.			
Depreciation of freezers.			
Checkout staff salaries.			
Flour used in in-store bakery.			

3.4 Cost classification by nature – direct and indirect

To make calculating a cost per unit easier costs are split into the following categories:

- A **direct** cost is an item of cost that is traceable directly to a cost unit.

  For example, the cost of a bought-in lights for a car manufacturer.

  The total of all direct costs is known as the "prime cost" per unit.

  An **indirect** cost is a cost that either cannot easily be identified with any one finished unit. Such costs are often referred to as "overheads".

  For example, the rent on a factory.

You may notice that we have used the term 'overheads' in two different ways in the last two sections – once to refer to **expenses** (costs other than labour and materials) and once to refer to **indirect costs** (costs that can't be traced to individual units of production). In reality there are some direct costs that are not materials or labour, but they fall outside the range of this exam. This means that, for our purposes, the term 'overhead' can be used to refer to either indirect costs **or** expenses.

 Activity 5

Chadwicks runs a car repair service and garage. Classify the following costs by nature (direct or indirect) in the table below.

Cost	Direct	Indirect
Engine oil used in services.		
Receptionist's wages.		
Annual repairs to engine crane.		
Brake pads.		

Activity 6

JJ Green is a furniture manufacturer. Classify the following costs by nature (direct or indirect) in the table below.

Cost	Direct	Indirect
Cost of wood and screws used.		
Royalty payable as a result of using a particular chair design.		
Oil used to lubricate the machines.		
Salesmen's salaries.		

3.5 Cost classification by behaviour – fixed and variable

For budgeting purposes, management needs to be able to predict **how costs will vary with differing levels of activity** (i.e. the number of cost units).

For example, if a furniture manufacturer expected to produce 1,000 chairs in a particular month, what should the budget for the costs of wood, labour, oil, selling costs, factory heat and light, manager's salaries, etc? How would these costs differ (if at all) if he expected to produce 2,000 chairs?

To make budgeting and forecasting easier, costs are split into the following categories:

- **Variable costs** are those that vary (usually assumed in direct proportion) with changes in level of activity

  For example, if you make twice the number of chairs then the amount (and hence the cost) of wood used would double.

- **Fixed costs** are not affected by changes in activity level.

  For example, the rent on the factory.

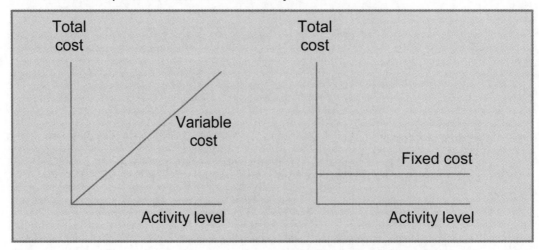

- **Semi-variable costs** are those that have a fixed element and a variable element.

  For example, the cost of electricity for the factory has a fixed element relating to lighting and a variable element relating to power used on the production line.

- **Stepped costs** are costs that remain fixed up to a particular level of activity, but which rise to a higher (fixed) level if activity goes beyond that range.

  For example, a firm may pay £40,000 per year to rent a factory in which they can produce up to 1 million units of product per year. However, if demand increases to more than 1 million units a second factory may be required, in which case the cost of factory rent may step up to, say, £80,000 per year and then be constant until we want to make 3 million.

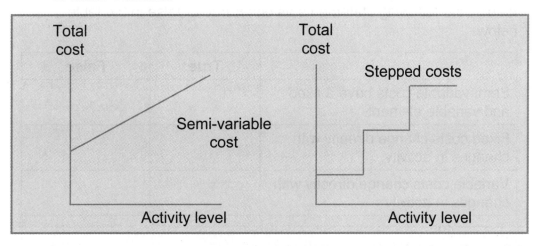

Activity 7

The Grande is a hotel in Wales. Classify the following costs by their behaviour in the table below.

Cost	Fixed	Variable	Semi-variable
Manager's salary.			
Cleaning materials.			
Food served in the restaurant.			
Electricity – includes a standing charge.			
Cleaner's wages (paid per room cleaned).			

Activity 8

Which of the following best describes a 'pure' fixed cost?

A cost which:

A   represents a fixed proportion of total costs

B   remains at the same level up to a particular level of output

C   has a direct relationship with output

D   remains at the same level whenever output changes

 Activity 9

Identify the following statements as either true or false in the table below.

	True	False
Semi-variable costs have a fixed and variable element.		
Fixed costs change directly with changes in activity.		
Variable costs change directly with changes in activity.		

3.6 Combining cost classifications

In some tasks in your assessment you may have to use more than one classification at a time. For example,

- Factory rent is a production cost that is fixed (or stepped) and indirect.

- Direct materials are a production cost that is also variable.

- Direct labour is not necessarily a variable cost. For a car repair service, for example, it is possible to identify how much time a particular repair takes (by using job cards to record time) but the mechanic may be on a fixed salary per month.

- Sales commission is a variable selling and distribution cost.

> ### 📝 Activity 10
>
> Identify the following statements as either true or false in the table below.
>
> | | True | False |
> |---|---|---|
> | All direct costs are variable. | | |
> | All overheads are fixed. | | |
> | Depreciation is always classified as an administrative cost. | | |
> | All selling costs are fixed. | | |

3.7 Why do organisations need to classify costs in different ways?

As you have seen in the previous sections, costs can be classified by nature, element, behaviour, or by function. Why do organisations need these different classifications?

The answer is that the different classifications will be used by the organisation for different purposes.

- **Classifying costs by element or nature** (materials, labour or overheads/direct and indirect costs) will be particularly useful for management accountants to help the business calculate how much each unit of product has cost to make. This can help the business decide how much to sell the product for.

- **Classifying costs by behaviour** (fixed, variable, stepped or semi-variable) will also be of use to management accountants, especially for the purpose of budgeting what the business' costs will be in future periods. For instance, if the business expects to double the number of units it makes next year, it will know that this will not affect the level of fixed costs, but would expect to double variable costs.

- **Classifying costs by function** (production, selling and distribution or administration) is of particular use to financial accountants, as it will help them to see the overall level of expenditure in each part of the organisation and therefore calculate total profit levels. This will then form part of the organisation's year-end financial accounts – in particular the income statement.

4 Summary

In this introductory chapter we looked at some of the basic principles and terminology used in cost and management accounting. Costs can be classified in a variety of different ways for different purposes.

The basic classification is into materials, labour and expenses, each of which will be dealt with in detail in the following chapters.

A further method of classification of costs is between direct and indirect costs. You need to be aware of the difference between cost units (individual units of a product or service for which costs can be separately ascertained) and cost centres (locations or functions in respect of which costs are accumulated).

For decision-making and budgeting purposes, it is often useful to distinguish costs according to their behaviour as production levels change. The basic classifications according to behaviour are fixed and variable costs although there are also stepped costs and semi-variable costs.

Answers to chapter activities

Activity 1

Characteristic	Financial accounting	Management accounting
Content can include anything useful.		☑
To help managers run the business.		☑
Formats dictated by accounting rules.	☑	
Looks mainly at historical information.	☑	
Produced for shareholders.	☑	

Activity 2

Student hours	=	Cost unit
Computer room and library	=	Cost centres

Activity 3

Cost	Production	Admin	Distribution
Purchases of plastic to make phone cases.	☑		
IT director's bonus.		☑	
Depreciation of factory building.	☑		
Salaries of production workers.	☑		
Insurance of sales team laptops.			☑

Activity 4

Cost	Materials	Labour	Overheads
Tins of baked beans.	☑		
Lighting costs.			☑
Depreciation of freezers.			☑
Checkout staff salaries.		☑	
Flour used in in-store bakery.	☑		

Activity 5

Cost	Direct	Indirect
Engine oil used in services.	☑	
Receptionist's wages.		☑
Annual repairs to engine crane.		☑
Brake pads.	☑	

Activity 6

Cost	Direct	Indirect
Cost of wood and screws used.	☑	
Royalty payable as a result of using a particular chair design.	☑	
Oil used to lubricate the machines.		☑
Salesmen's salaries.		☑

Note: You may have argued that oil was direct as you could calculate how much oil is needed per item made. However, it would be very difficult to determine the oil need for a **particular** item of furniture; hence the correct answer is indirect.

Activity 7

Cost	Fixed	Variable	Semi-variable
Manager's salary.	☑		
Cleaning materials.		☑	
Food in restaurant.		☑	
Electricity – includes a standing charge.			☑
Cleaner's wages (paid per room cleaned).		☑	

Activity 8

D – Pure fixed costs remain exactly the same in total regardless of the activity level.

Activity 9

	True	False
Semi-variable costs have a fixed and variable element.	☑	
Fixed costs change directly with changes in activity.		☑
Variable costs change directly with changes in activity.	☑	

Activity 10

	True	False
All direct costs are variable		☑ Note 1
All overheads are fixed		☑ Note 2
Depreciation is always classified as an administrative cost		☑ Note 3
All selling costs are fixed		☑ Note 4

Note 1: Whereas direct materials are usually variable, direct labour may be fixed – e.g. lawyers may be on a fixed salary but produce detailed timesheets so a direct labour cost can be calculated for each client.

Note 2: Electricity is usually classified as an overhead but will have a variable element. If more units are made on a production line, then more electricity will be used (hence variable). However, it may not be possible or practical to measure exactly how much electricity is used to make a particular unit (hence indirect).

Note 3: For example, depreciation on production machinery would be included in cost of sales.

Note 4: Sales commission would be a variable selling cost.

5 Test your knowledge

Workbook Activity 11

The table below lists some of the characteristics of financial accounting and management accounting systems. Indicate the characteristics for each system by putting a tick in the relevant column of the table.

Characteristic	Financial accounting	Management accounting
Content can include forecasts.		
Looks mainly at historical information.		
Format must conform to statute and accounting standards.		
Any format can be used.		
Mainly produced to help managers run and control the business.		
Would be used by potential investors thinking of buying shares.		
Produced for shareholders.		

Workbook Activity 12

Zenawi plc makes garden furniture.

Classify the following costs by function in the table below.

Cost	Production	Admin	Distribution
Purchases of wood to make chairs.			
Depreciation of delivery vans.			
HR director's bonus.			
Salaries of production workers.			
Electricity bill for workshop.			
Insurance of sales team laptops.			

 Workbook Activity 13

Kim and Yoshiro are the founding partners of an accountancy firm. They employ 20 accountants and have over 100 clients.

Classify the following costs by nature (direct or indirect) in the table below.

Cost	Direct	Indirect
Travelling costs for when staff visit clients.		
Rechargeable accountants' time.		
Office heating costs.		
Recruitment costs.		
Accountants' time recorded as "general admin." on time sheets.		

Workbook Activity 14

Elite Cars is a family-run business specialising in the sale, hire, servicing and repair of classic cars.

Classify the following costs by their behaviour in the table below.

Cost	Fixed	Variable	Semi-variable
Sales staff pay.			
Motor oil used in servicing.			
Depreciation of premises.			
Mechanics' pay (salaried).			
Electricity.			

Coding of costs and income

Introduction

This chapter looks at the use of coding in organisations, including how income and expenditure is coded.

KNOWLEDGE
2.1 Explain how materials, labour and expenses are classified and recorded
2.2 Explain different methods of coding

SKILLS
2.3 Classify and code cost information for materials, labour and expenses

CONTENTS

1   Classification and coding of costs
2   Coding in practice
3   Problems with coding

1 Classification and coding of costs

Cost accountants need to determine the costs that relate to each cost or profit centre. To make this simpler, each expense is classified according to its cost centre and type of expense.

A cost code is then allocated to the expense to represent this classification.

1.1 Coding systems

 Definition

A **code** is a system of symbols designed to be applied to a classified set of items, to give a brief, accurate reference, which helps entry to the records, collation and analysis.

A cost code is a code used in a costing system.

1.2 Cost codes

In general, cost codes are constructed by deciding on the information that is needed. For most businesses we want to identify

(a)　the profit or cost centre that is incurring the cost and

(b)　the type of cost that is incurred.

There are no set methods of designing a cost code and the cost code of a particular organisation will be that which best suits the operations and costs of that business.

For example, if a business has only one division/operating centre, then there will be no need to identify that centre in the cost code. But if a business has several divisions, then the division that incurs the cost will need to be identified in the cost code.

Similarly, if the divisions have several cost centres and incur several different types of cost, then the cost code must be able to identify each of these.

There are a number of different methods of coding data:

*   **numeric:** e.g. 100/310
*   **alphabetic**: e.g. AB/RT
*   **alpha-numeric**: e.g. A230

Example

Consider a company that has two operating divisions (North and South), two cost centres in each division (Construction and Despatch) with each cost centre incurring three types of cost (material, labour and expenses)

A typical cost code could be devised as follows

Step 1   Decide the structure of the cost code, for example **/**/**, where

First two digits   the operating division
Second two digits   the cost centre
Third two digits   the type of cost

Step 2   Allocate code numbers to the elements

(a)   two operating divisions

North   01

South   02

(b)   each division has two cost centres

Construction   01

Despatch   02

(c)   each cost centre incurs three types of cost

Materials   01

Labour   02

Expense   03

Examples

Thus a cost code for expenses incurred by the despatch centre of the North division would be:

First two digits	the operating division	North	01
Second two digits	the cost centre	Despatch	02
Third two digits	the type of cost	Expenses	03

The cost code would therefore be: 01/02/03

Similarly, the code for materials purchased by the construction centre of the South would be 02/01/01.

1.3   More complex codes

Once a cost has been allocated its correct cost centre code then it may also be useful to know the particular type of expense involved. Therefore some more digits might be added to the cost centre code to represent the precise type of cost.

Example

If an expense for Machine Group 7 is for oil then its code might be 07 (for its cost centre) followed by 23 to represent materials followed by 04 to represent oil.

If an expense of the canteen is identified as frozen peas then its cost code might be 16 (its cost centre) followed by 02 to represent food purchases (materials) followed by 19 to represent frozen peas.

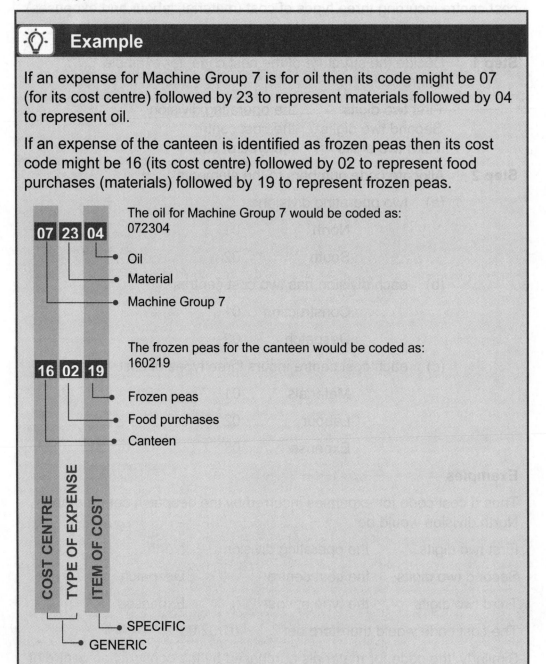

The oil for Machine Group 7 would be coded as:
072304

07 23 04

- Oil
- Material
- Machine Group 7

The frozen peas for the canteen would be coded as:
160219

16 02 19

- Frozen peas
- Food purchases
- Canteen

COST CENTRE
TYPE OF EXPENSE
ITEM OF COST

- SPECIFIC
- GENERIC

Activity 1

Greggs Ltd, a manufacturer of garden lighting, uses a numerical coding structure based on one profit centre and three cost centres as outlined below. Each code has a sub-code so each transaction will be coded as ***/***.

Profit/cost centre	Code	Sub-classification	Sub-code
Sales	100	Sales to the public	100
		Sales to retailers	200
Production	200	Direct costs	100
		Indirect costs	200
Selling and distribution	300	Direct costs	100
		Indirect costs	200
Administration	400	Direct costs	100
		Indirect costs	200

Code the following revenue and expense transactions, which have been extracted from purchase invoices, sales invoices and payroll, using the table below.

Transaction	Code
Wages for staff working in the factory canteen.	
Sales to a French retailer.	
Sales to individuals via the company website.	
Depreciation on cars provided to salesmen.	
Bulbs for use in the garden lighting products.	
Chief accountant's salary.	

Activity 2

Owen Ltd manufactures motorbike helmets.

It has two factories that are coded as:

Slough	S
Leeds	L

Each factory has the following cost centres:

Machining	120
Finishing	121
Packing	122
Stores	123
Canteen	124
Maintenance	125
Administration	126

Type of expense:

Labour	200
Material	201
Expenses	202

Sales revenue: 210

Thus, the cost of production labour in the Finishing Department at the Leeds factory would be coded L/121/200.

Code the following expenses using the table below.

Transaction	Code
Slough factory, cleaning materials used in the canteen.	
Slough factory, wages for stores personnel.	
Leeds factory, electricity for Machining Department.	
Leeds factory, telephone account for site as a whole.	
Slough factory, general maintenance material for repairs.	

Activity 3

Jeff plc manufactures computer printers and wishes to start coding its costs. It has decided to use an alphabetic code, based on the nature and the element of each cost, as well as the function it relates to.

The first part of the code will depend on whether the cost is direct or indirect.

Direct	J
Indirect	F

The second part of the code will depend on whether the cost is materials, labour or expenses (overheads).

Labour	HF
Materials	MB
Expenses	VV

The third part of the code will depend on the function that the cost relates to.

Production	PR
Administration	AD
Sales and distribution	SD

Thus, the cost of indirect production materials would be coded F/MB/PR

Code the following expenses using the table below.

Transaction	Code
Purchase of plastic used in the production of printers.	
Electricity used in Jeff's administration head office.	
Wages paid to the cleaner of Jeff's delivery vans.	
Purchase of ink for the head office printers.	
Salary paid to Jeff's factory supervisor.	

1.4 Purpose of cost codes

The main purposes of cost codes are to:

- **assist precise information:** costs incurred can be associated with pre-established codes, so reducing variations in classification

- **facilitate electronic data processing:** computer analysis, summarisation and presentation of data can be performed more easily through the use of codes

- **facilitate a logical and systematic arrangement of costing records:** accounts can be arranged in blocks of codes permitting additional codes to be inserted in logical order

- **simplify comparison of totals of similar expenses** rather than all of the individual items

- **incorporate check codes** within the main code to check the accuracy of the postings.

2 Coding in practice

2.1 Timing of coding

In order to be of most use the coding of costs should take place when the cost or expense is first received by the organisation. In most cases this will be when the invoice for the goods is received.

After this point the documents will be entered into the accounting system and then to the filing system so it is important that the coding is done immediately.

2.2 Receiving an invoice

When an invoice is received by the organisation it will undergo a variety of checks to ensure that it is for valid purchases that were ordered and have been received or that it is for a service that has been received.

In the process of these checks it will become clear what type of goods or service is being dealt with, for example it may be an invoice for the purchase of raw materials for the factory or an electricity bill for the entire organisation.

Once the invoice has been checked for validity then it must be correctly coded.

2.3 Choosing the correct code

In order for the correct code to be given to the invoice, it is vital that the person responsible for the coding fully understands the nature of the organisation and the costs that it incurs. The organisation's coding listing should be referred to and the correct cost centre, type and expense code should be entered on the front of the invoice.

2.4 Cheque and cash payments

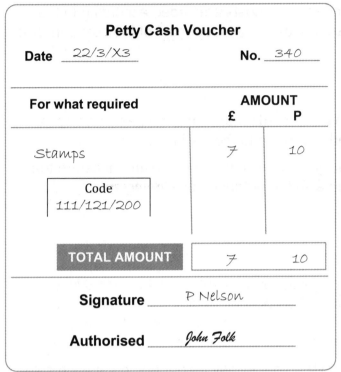

Petty Cash Voucher

Date _____22/3/X3_____   No. ___340___

For what required	AMOUNT	
	£	P
Stamps	7	10
Code 111/121/200		
TOTAL AMOUNT	7	10

Signature _____P Nelson_____

Authorised _____John Folk_____

As well as receiving invoices for costs incurred on credit most organisations will also write cheques for costs and even pay some costs out of petty cash. These costs must be coded in just the same way as purchases or expenses on credit.

If the payment is by cheque then there will be some documentation to support that payment. When this documentation is authorised for payment then it should also be coded for costing purposes.

If payments are made out of petty cash then they must be supported by a petty cash voucher. Again this voucher must be coded according to the type of cost.

2.5 Shared costs

Shared costs are costs that do not relate specifically to a particular cost centre. Some costs, for example electricity bills, cannot be allocated directly to a single cost centre as they are indirect costs which relate to a number of cost centres. Eventually a portion of this electricity bill will be shared out to each of the cost centres that uses electricity but at the point where the account is being coded it must simply be recognised that this is a shared cost and not a cost that should be coded to a particular cost centre.

Therefore, the coding structure of the organisation should include some codes that specifically identify a cost as a shared cost.

2.6 Payment of wages and salaries

Wages and salaries normally form a very large part of the costs incurred by an organisation. If wages or salaries are paid by cheque or in cash then the supporting documentation, the payslip, should be coded as with other cash payments.

However frequently wages and salaries will usually be paid directly into employee's bank accounts through the BACS system. Therefore it is important that the wages and salaries costs are coded according to the department or cost centre so that the total labour cost of the cost centre is known.

2.7 Sales invoices

If an organisation makes sales on credit then when the sales invoice is produced it should be coded according to the coding listing.

This code will probably specify the profit centre or investment centre that has made the sale and often also the product that is being sold.

2.8 Cash sales

In a retail organisation sales may be made for cash.

There should always be documentation that supports the cash takings, such as the till rolls for the day. This documentation then needs to be coded to reflect the profit or investment centre that made the sales and any other detailed product coding that is required by the organisation.

Most modern cash registers will automatically record and code each sale using the bar code on the product.

2.9 Assets and liabilities

We have concentrated so far on the costing of costs and revenue. However there are other items that also need to be coded, for example assets and liabilities.

The sort of assets that may occur in the exam are fixed assets (or "non-current assets") purchased for the business and current assets (for example, debtors or "receivables").

Example

Codebreaker Ltd manufactures the Enigma game machine.

The company has bought a production machine for £5,000.

The coding system is structured as:

- First two digits refer to the profit centre (the Enigma machine is profit centre 08).

- The additional code digits for fixed assets for production are 2600.

The code for the expenditure made by purchasing the machine are

    £5,000   082600

These codes would be the instruction to the accountant (or the computer) to post £5,000 to the appropriate fixed asset account.

3 Problems with coding

3.1 Which code?

The main problem when coding documents is deciding which cost centre and analysis code to use; the documents may not clearly show which cost centre incurred the costs or the type of cost it is.

If you are unable to code a document try:

- looking in the organisation's procedures manual

- referring the query document to your supervisor.

3.2 Apportionment

As mentioned above, if more than one cost centre has incurred the cost (for example, a heating bill for the whole building), the cost needs to be shared between all of the cost centres (or apportioned).

Although it may be easy to simply share the costs equally between the cost centres, some cost centres may be bigger than others and therefore use more electricity/heating etc – so should receive a greater percentage of the cost.

You will learn more about methods of cost apportionment in the level 3 unit 'Costs and revenues'.

4 Summary

You should now know the importance of coding of costs and income. If actual costs and income are to be used for management purposes then it is vital that they are correctly classified and coded to ensure that they are allocated to the correct cost, profit or investment centre and according to the correct type of costs – material, labour or expense. Only then can any useful management information be obtained.

Answers to chapter activities

Activity 1

Transaction	Code
Wages for staff working in the factory canteen.	200/200
Sales to a French retailer.	100/200
Sales to individuals via the company website.	100/100
Depreciation on cars provided to salesmen.	300/200
Bulbs for use in the garden lighting products.	200/100
Chief accountant's salary.	400/200

Activity 2

Transaction	Code
Slough factory, cleaning materials used in the canteen.	S/124/201
Slough factory, wages for stores personnel.	S/123/200
Leeds factory, electricity for Machining Department.	L/120/202
Leeds factory, telephone account for site as a whole.	L/126/202
Slough factory, general maintenance material for repairs.	S/125/201

✏️ **Activity 3**	

Transaction	Code
Purchase of plastic used in the production of printers.	J/MB/PR
Electricity used in Jeff's administration head office.	F/VV/AD
Wages paid to the cleaner of Jeff's delivery vans.	F/HF/SD
Purchase of ink for the head office printers.	F/MB/AD
Salary paid to Jeff's factory supervisor.	F/HF/PR

5 Test your knowledge

Workbook Activity 4

A company manufactures shoes and slippers in half-sizes in the following size ranges:

- Men's 6 to 9½
- Ladies 3 to 9
- Boys 1 to 5½
- Girls 1 to 5

The company uses a seven-digit code to identify its finished products, which, reading from left to right, is built up as follows:

Digit one indicates whether the products are mens, ladies, boys or girls. The numbers used are

1 – mens

2 – ladies

3 – boys

4 – girls

Digit two denotes type of footwear (3 is shoes; 6 is slippers)

Digit three denotes colour (5 is green; 6 is burgundy, 1 is brown)

Digit four denotes the material of the upper part of the product (leather is 4)

Digit five denotes the material of the sole (leather is 1)

Digits six and seven denote size.

Example

Code 1613275 represents a pair of Men's slippers, brown suede, rubber sole, size 7½

Task: Set suitable code numbers to the following:

Product	Code
Boys' shoes, brown leather uppers, rubber soles, size 4.	
Ladies' slippers, green suede uppers, rubber soles, size 4½.	
Girls' shoes, burgundy leather uppers, leather soles, size 3½.	

Workbook Activity 5

The expenses of an international organisation are coded with a seven digit code system as follows:

First and second digits	–	location
Third and fourth digits	–	function
Final three digits	–	type of expense

Extracts from within the costing system are as follows:

Location	Code		Function	Code
London	10		Production	20
Dublin	11		Marketing	21
Lagos	12		Accounts	23
Nairobi	13		Administration	24
Kuala Lumpur	17			
Hong Kong	18		**Type of expense**	**Code**
			Factory rent	201
			Stationery	202
			Telephone	203
			Travel	204
			Entertainment	205

Examples of the codes are as follows:

Factory rent in Nairobi: 1320201
Stationery purchased in London office: 1024202

Task

Code the following revenue and expense transactions, which have been extracted from purchase invoices, sales invoices and payroll, using the table below.

Transaction	Code
Factory rent in the Dublin factory.	
Administration telephone costs incurred in Lagos.	
Salesman in Hong Kong entertaining an overseas visitor.	
Marketing brochures ordered in London.	

Materials and inventory

3

Introduction

This chapter considers in more detail materials, the different types of inventory and how inventories are valued and classified.

KNOWLEDGE

2.1 Explain how materials, labour and expenses are classified and recorded.

2.4 Classify different types of inventory as: raw materials, part-finished goods (work-in-progress), finished goods

2.6 Explain different methods of inventory valuation

SKILLS

2.5 Calculate inventory valuations and issues of inventory using these methods: First in first out (FIFO), Last in first out (LIFO), Weighted Average (AVCO).

CONTENTS

1   Different types of inventory
2   Valuing raw materials
3   Valuing WIP and finished goods
4   The materials purchasing cycle in practice

1 Different types of inventory

1.1 The production cycle

For a retailer the main type of inventory will be goods bought for resale.

For a manufacturer, however, we can identify three types of inventory:

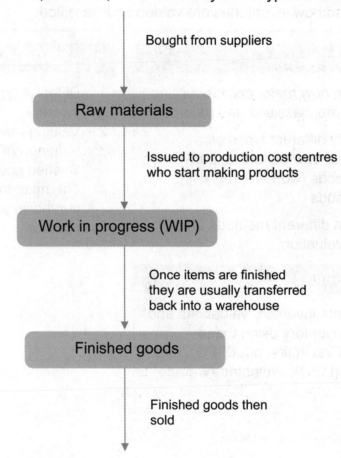

Bought from suppliers

Raw materials

Issued to production cost centres
who start making products

Work in progress (WIP)

Once items are finished
they are usually transferred
back into a warehouse

Finished goods

Finished goods then
sold

You may also see "inventory" referred to as "stock".

1.2 Materials

For manufacturers various materials are needed to make the main product
of the business.

Remember that, for management accounting purposes, costs can be
classified as either direct or indirect. Materials are no exception to this.

Definition

Direct materials are the materials that are used directly as part of the production of the goods that the organisation makes.

The direct materials are therefore the raw materials that are part of the manufacturing process. In a business that makes wooden furniture the direct materials would for example include wood, hinges and polish.

 Definition

Indirect materials are other materials used in the production process which are not used in the actual products themselves.

So for example lubricant for the machines that make the wooden furniture would be classified as indirect materials as it would be extremely difficult to identify how much lubricant was used to make a particular chair, say.

 Definition

The total **direct** cost for a product (the direct materials and direct labour costs of producing it) is sometimes referred to as the **prime cost**.

1.3 Work in progress

Work in progress (WIP) refers to units that have been started but are incomplete at the end of the accounting period.

For example a wooden table may have had the top made but is still waiting for legs to be attached.

1.4 Finished goods

Finished goods are completed and ready for selling to customers.

2 Valuing raw materials

2.1 Introduction

There are two aspects to valuing raw materials:

- Firstly we need to determine the cost of materials issued to production cost centres.

- Secondly we need to be able to value the inventory of raw materials left in stores.

The cost of materials purchased will normally be derived from suppliers' invoices but, where many purchases have been made at differing prices, a decision has to be taken as to which cost is used when inventory is issued to the user department (cost centre).

Example

Petra Ltd has the following movements in a certain type of inventory into and out of it stores for the month of May:

Date	Receipts			Issues	
	Kg	Price/kg	Cost	Kg	Cost
May 1	200	£9.00	£1,800		
May 2	100	£10.80	£1,080		
May 3				50	?

What is the cost of materials issued on May 3?

Should we use £9/kg, £10.80/kg or something in between?

2.2 Methods of pricing issues of materials

Various methods exist including:

(a) FIFO (first in, first out)

(b) LIFO (last in, first out)

(c) Weighed average (AVCO)

The choice of method will not only affect the charge to the user department for which the material is required, but also the value of the inventory left in stores.

These systems attempt to reflect the movements of individual units in and out of inventory under different assumptions.

- **FIFO** – assumes that issues will be made from the oldest inventory available, leaving the latest purchases in inventory. This means that transfers from stores to production will be made at the oldest prices and the newest prices will be used to value the remaining inventory.

  FIFO is particularly useful when products are perishable and you want the oldest used first to avoid it going off or becoming out of date e.g. milk .

- **LIFO** – assumes that issues will be made from the newest inventory available, leaving the earliest purchases in inventory. This means that transfers from stores to production will be made at the newest prices and the older prices will be used to value the remaining inventory.

  LIFO could be used when products are not perishable e.g. stationery

- **AVCO** – assumes that the issues into production will be made at an average price. This is calculated by taking the total value of the inventory and dividing it by the total units in inventory, thus finding the average price per unit. A new average cost is calculated before each issue to production.

  AVCO could be used when individual units of material are not separately definable e.g. sand at a builders merchants.

Example – continued

Petra Ltd has the following movements in a certain type of inventory into and out of it stores for the month of May:

Date	Receipts			Issues	
	Kg	Price/kg	Cost	Kg	Cost
May 1	200	£9.00	£1,800		
May 2	100	£10.80	£1,080		
May 3				50	

Complete the table below for the issue and closing inventory values.

Method	Cost of issue	Closing inventory
FIFO		
LIFO		
AVCO		

Solution

Method	Cost of issue	Closing inventory
FIFO	£450	£2,430
LIFO	£540	£2,340
AVCO	£480	£2,400

Workings

FIFO

- The 50 kg issued on May 3rd will all come from the **earliest** purchase made on May 1st.

- Thus the cost of the issue will be 50 kg @ 9 = £450

- There are two ways to get closing inventory.

- The first is to look at the flow of units : closing inventory will be 150 kg @ £9 (the remaining inventory from the May 1st purchase) and 100 kg @ £10.80 = £2,430

- The second approach, which will probably be easier in the exam, is to consider total purchases and simply deduct issues. Total purchases = £2,880, so closing inventory = 2,880 – 450 = £2,430

LIFO

- The 50 kg issued on May 3rd will all come from the **most recent** purchase made on May 2nd.

- Thus the cost of the issue will be 50 kg @ £10.80 = £540

- Closing inventory = 2,880 – 540 = £2,340

- **OR** closing inventory will be 200 kg @ £9 (May 1st purchase) and 50 kg @ £10.80 (the remaining inventory from May 2nd) = £2,340

AVCO

- We bought 300 kg at a total cost of 200 @ £9 + 100 @ £10.80 = £2,880

- On average this works out at 2,880/300 = £9.60/kg

- Thus the cost of the issue will be 50 kg @ 9.60 = £480

- Closing inventory = 2,880 – 480 = £2,400

- **OR** closing inventory carried forwards will have the same average cost per unit so will be 250 kg @ £9.60 = £2,400

Activity 1

Krully Ltd has the following movements in a certain type of inventory into and out of it stores for the month of June:

Date	Receipts		Issues	
	Units	Cost	Units	Cost
June 2	100	£400		
June 3	200	£1,000		
June 6	200	£1,200		
June 19			400	
June 25	400	£2,500		

Complete the table below for the issue and closing inventory values.

Method	Cost of issue on 19 June	Closing inventory at 30 June
FIFO		
LIFO		
AVCO		

 Activity 2

Jetty Ltd has opening inventory of raw material X of 1,500 units at £2 per unit. In the month another 1,000 units at £4.50 are received and the following week 1,800 units are issued.

Identify whether the statements in the table below are true or false by putting a tick in the relevant column.

Statement	True	False
FIFO values the closing inventory at £1,400.		
LIFO costs the issue at £6,100.		
AVCO costs the issue at £5,400.		

2.3 Determining which method of inventory valuation has been used

You may be given a completed or partially completed inventory card and asked to decide which of the three methods have been used to produce it.

 Example

JJJ Ltd has the following movements in a certain type of inventory into and out of it stores for the month of June:

Date	Receipts			Issues	
	Kg	Price/kg	Cost	Kg	Cost
June 1	500	£5.00	£2,500		
June 2	700	£6.00	£4,200		
June 3				900	£4,900

Identify the method JJJ has used to value its inventory and calculate the valuation of closing inventory using this method.

Solution

Method	Closing inventory
FIFO	£1,800

Workings

The most reliable way of tackling this question is to look at the cost calculation that has been done for you – in this case the cost of the issue on June 3rd. If we calculate what this issue would be worth under each of the three valuation methods, we should be able to identify the approach that JJJ has taken.

LIFO

- The 900 kg issued on June 3rd will all come from the **most recent** purchases made.

- Thus the cost of the issue will be (700 kg @ £6) + (200 kg @ £5) = £5,200.

- As the cost of the issue is £4,900, the method being used is not LIFO.

AVCO

- We bought 1,200 kg at a total cost of (500 kg @ £5) + (700 kg @ £6) = £6,700

- On average this works out at £6,700/1,200 = £5.58/kg

- Thus the cost of the issue will be 900 kg @ £5.58/kg = £5,022

As the cost of the issue is £4,900, the method being used is not AVCO.

FIFO

- The 900 kg issued on June 3rd will all come from the **earliest** purchases.

- Thus the cost of the issue will be (500 kg @ £5) + (400 kg @ £6) = £4,900. As this is the value of the issue given, FIFO must be the valuation method used.

- Remember that there are two ways to get closing inventory.

- The first is to look at the flow of units : closing inventory will be 300 kg @ £6 (the remaining inventory from the June 2nd purchase)

- The second approach, which will probably be easier in the exam, is to consider total purchases and simply deduct issues. Total purchases = £6,700, so closing inventory = £6,700 – £4,900 = £1,800.

 Activity 3

Flotsam Ltd has opening inventory of raw material P of 3,000 units at £4.50 per unit. In the month another 2,000 units at £7 are received and the following week 3,750 units are issued.

Identify the valuation method described in the statements below by putting a tick in the relevant column.

Statement	FIFO	LIFO	AVCO
The closing inventory is valued at £6,875.			
The issue of 3,750 units is costed at £18,750			
The issue of 3,750 units is costed at £21,875			

2.4 Features of the different methods

FIFO is fairly easy to understand and has the following features:

- In times of rapidly increasing prices, material may be issued at an early and hence unrealistically low price, resulting in the particular job showing an unusually large profit.

- Two jobs started on the same day may show a different cost for the same quantity of the same material.

- In times of rapidly increasing prices FIFO will give a higher profit figure than LIFO or AVCO.

LIFO is also fairly simple to follow and has the following features:

- In contrast to FIFO closing inventories will now be shown at the earliest prices which means that in times of rapidly increasing or decreasing prices, the inventory figure bears little resemblance to the current cost of replacement.

- As with FIFO, two jobs started on the same day may show a different cost for the same quantity of the same material.

- The LIFO method uses the latest prices for issues to production and therefore the cost obtained is more likely to be in line with other costs and selling prices.

- In times of rapidly increasing prices LIFO will give a lower profit figure than FIFO and AVCO.

AVCO is a compromise on valuation of inventory and issues and the average price rarely reflects the actual purchase price of the material.

 Activity 4

Identify the correct inventory valuation method from the characteristic given by putting a tick in the relevant column of the table below.

Characteristic	FIFO	LIFO	AVCO
• Issues are valued at the most recent purchase cost.			
• Inventory is valued at the average of the cost of purchases.			
• Inventory is valued at the most recent purchase cost.			

Activity 5

Identify the following statements as either true or false.

Statement	True	False
• FIFO costs issues of inventory at the most recent purchase price.		
• AVCO costs issues of inventory at the oldest purchase price.		
• LIFO costs issues of inventory at the oldest purchase price.		
• FIFO values closing inventory at the most recent purchase price.		
• LIFO values closing inventory at the most recent purchase price.		
• AVCO values closing inventory at the latest purchase price.		

3 Valuing WIP and finished goods

3.1 Basic principles

When valuing WIP or finished goods we need to incorporate all the different costs incurred to bring it to its present location and condition. To make this easier, direct costs are included first and then indirect costs or overheads added.

Identifying direct materials and labour should be straightforward, or the costs would not be classified as "direct":

- Direct materials could be identified using job cards and information on stores requisitions.

- Direct labour can be identified using job cards and time sheets.

Because it is more difficult to identify overheads with units of output some system needs to be developed for either averaging overheads over units or absorbing them into units. This is particularly important when a company makes more than one product.

This is discussed in more detail in the "Costs and Revenues" unit but here you need to be aware of two approaches:

- Unit basis – each unit gets the same level of overhead.

- Labour rate basis – here overheads are absorbed as a rate per direct labour hour. This means that for every hour someone works on the unit an hour's worth of overhead is given to the unit as well.

Example

The cost per unit for completed goods could show the following:

	Unit cost £
Direct labour cost (2 hours @£10/hour)	20
Direct material cost	3
Direct expenses	1
Prime cost	24
Production overheads (2 hours @ £4/hour)	8
Total cost per unit	32

Example

A job card showing the WIP on job number 217 might look like the following:

JOB NO	217		
Materials requisitions	**Quantity**	**£**	**Total (£)**
0254 G 3578	100 kg	4,200	
0261 K 3512	50 kg	3,150	
			7,350
Wages – employees	**Hours**	**£**	
13343	80	656	
15651	30	300	
12965	40	360	
	150		1,316
Overheads	**Hours**	**£**	
Absorption rate £12	150	1,800	1,800
Total cost			10,466

3.2 Calculating a cost per unit

In the exam you may be asked to calculate a unit cost at a specified production level. When doing this, be careful to distinguish between fixed and variable costs and do not confuse total costs and unit costs.

Example

Baker Ltd is costing a single product which has the following cost details

Variable Costs per unit

Materials	£5
Labour	£6
Total fixed costs	£70,000

Complete the following total cost and unit cost table for a production level of 20,000 units.

Element	Total cost	Unit cost
Materials	£	£
Labour	£	£
Overheads	£	£
Total	£	£

Solution

Element	Total cost	Unit cost
Materials	£100,000	£5.00
Labour	£120,000	£6.00
Overheads	£70,000	£3.50
Total	£290,000	£14.50

Workings

Materials:

- This is a variable cost – unit cost is £5 (given)
- Total cost will be 20,000 × £5 = £100,000

Labour:

- This is a variable cost – unit cost is £6 (given)
- Total cost will be 20,000 × £6 = £120,000

Overheads

- This is a fixed cost – total cost is £70,000 (given)
- Unit cost will be 70,000 ÷ 20,000 = £3.50

 Activity 6

XYZ Ltd is costing a single product which has the following cost details

Variable costs per unit

Materials	£4
Labour	£5
Total fixed costs	£60,000

Complete the following total cost and unit cost table for a production level of 15,000 units.

Element	Total cost	Unit cost
Materials	£	£
Labour	£	£
Overheads	£	£
Total	£	£

Example

Complete the table below showing fixed costs, variable costs, total costs and unit cost at the different levels of production.

Units	Fixed costs	Variable costs	Total costs	Unit cost
1,000	£20,000	£4,000	£24,000	£24.00
2,000	£	£	£	£
3,000	£	£	£	£
4,000	£	£	£	£

Solution

Units	Fixed costs	Variable costs	Total costs	Unit cost
1,000	£20,000	£4,000	£24,000	£24.00
2,000	£20,000	£8,000	£28,000	£14.00
3,000	£20,000	£12,000	£32,000	£10.67
4,000	£20,000	£16,000	£36,000	£9.00

Workings

Fixed costs:

- Unless there are stepped costs, the fixed costs will be the same at each activity level.

Variable costs – approach 1

- Calculate the variable cost per unit = £4,000/1,000 units = £4 per unit.

- This can then be used to get the total variable cost at different levels.

- So for 3,000 units the total variable cost will be 3,000 × £4 = £12,000.

Variable costs – approach 2

- Alternatively you could scale up the total variable cost.
- For example, going from 1,000 to 3,000 units we have increased the number of units by a factor of 3 so need to do the same to the variable costs.
- This gives total variable cost = 3 × 4,000 = £12,000 as before.

Unit costs

- Simply divide the total cost by the number of units
- E.g. for 4,000 units, unit costs = £36,000/4,000 = £9 per unit.

 Activity 7

Complete the table below showing fixed costs, variable costs, total costs and unit cost at the different levels of production.

Units	Fixed costs	Variable costs	Total costs	Unit cost
1,000	£60,000	£2,000	£62,000	£62.00
2,000	£	£	£	£
3,000	£	£	£	£
4,000	£	£	£	£

3.3 Factory cost of goods sold

As well as valuing units for inventory purposes we also want to know the cost of goods sold. The main issue here is that we need to adjust the costs incurred within the period to take into account opening and closing inventory.

For a retailer:

Cost of sales = opening inventory + purchases – closing inventory

For a manufacturer there will be the further complication that there will be opening and closing inventories for raw materials, work in progress and finished goods. This could be shown as a full manufacturing account:

Example – Manufacturing account

	£
Opening inventory of raw materials	7,000
Purchases of raw materials	50,000
Closing inventory of raw materials	(10,000)
DIRECT MATERIALS USED	47,000
Direct labour	97,000
DIRECT COST	**144,000**
Manufacturing overheads	53,000
MANUFACTURING COST	**197,000**
Opening inventory of work in progress	8,000
Closing inventory of work in progress	(10,000)
COST OF GOODS MANUFACTURED	**195,000**
Opening inventory of finished goods	30,000
Closing inventory of finished goods	(25,000)
COST OF GOODS SOLD	**200,000**

Activity 8

Reorder the following costs into a manufacturing account format:

	£
Manufacturing overheads	47,000
Purchases of raw materials	60,000
MANUFACTURING COST	**147,000**
Opening inventory of raw materials	14,000
Closing inventory of finished goods	(70,000)
COST OF GOODS SOLD	**147,000**
DIRECT COST	**100,000**
Opening inventory of work in progress	42,000
DIRECT MATERIALS USED	64,000
Direct labour	36,000
Closing inventory of raw materials	(10,000)
Closing inventory of work in progress	(32,000)
COST OF GOODS MANUFACTURED	**157,000**
Opening inventory of finished goods	60,000

4 The materials purchasing cycle in practice

4.1 Introduction

Materials can often form the largest single item of cost for a business so it is essential that the material purchased is the most suitable for the intended purpose.

4.2 Control of purchasing

When goods are purchased they must be ordered, received by the stores department, recorded, issued to the manufacturing department that requires them and eventually paid for. This process needs a great deal of paperwork and strict internal controls.

Internal control consists of full documentation and appropriate authorisation of all transactions, movements of materials and of all requisitions, orders, receipts and payments.

If control is to be maintained over purchasing, it is necessary to ensure that:

- only necessary items are purchased

- orders are placed with the most appropriate supplier after considering price and delivery details

- the goods that are actually received are the goods that were ordered and in the correct quantity

- the price paid for the goods is correct (i.e. what was agreed when the order was placed).

To ensure that all of this takes place requires a reliable system of checking and control.

4.3   Overview of procedures

It is useful to have an overview of the purchasing process.

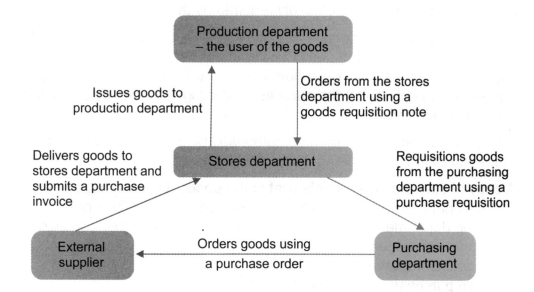

There are many variations of the above system in practice, but it is a fairly typical system and does provide good control over the purchasing and issuing process.

 Activity 9 (no feedback)

Your organisation may have a slightly different process to this. See if you can draw a similar diagram illustrating the way your organisation's (or a familiar organisation's) purchasing process works.

4.4 Purchase orders

Purchase orders will be sent to suppliers by the purchasing department. The choice of supplier will depend upon the price, delivery promise, quality of goods and past performance.

The person placing the order must first check that the purchase requisition has been authorised by the appropriate person in the organisation, as a check that the goods are genuinely required by the organisation.

Once the supplier of the goods has been chosen, the purchase price of the goods must be determined. This will either be from the price list of the supplier or from a special quotation of the price by that supplier. The price agreed will be entered on the purchase order together with details of the goods being ordered.

The purchase order must then be authorised by the appropriate person in the organisation before being dispatched to the supplier.

A copy of the purchase order is sent to the goods receiving department or stores department as confirmation of expected delivery. The goods receiving department therefore know that goods are due and can alert appropriate management if they are not received. A copy is also sent to the accounts department to be matched to the supplier's invoice. An example purchase order is shown overleaf.

Example

BLACKHILL FILES
742 St Anne's Way, York YO5 4NP
Telephone 01904 27635
Registered in England, No 1457893

PURCHASE ORDER

Printing Unlimited   Order No: 35762
80 New High Street
Exeter   Ref: T. Holmes
EX4 2LP

Date: 22 June 20X4

Please print 25,000 labels at £10.50 per 1,000.
Needed by 20 July 20X4.
Payment within 30 days of delivery.
2% early settlement discount.

Delivery to: As above

4.5 Purchase invoice

The supplier will submit a purchase invoice for goods detailing the amount that we must pay for them and the date that payment is due. The purchase invoice might be included when the goods themselves are delivered, or might be sent after delivery.

The purchase invoice is the primary source of information for recording the quantity and cost of materials purchased.

The person responsible for payment must check that the details of the purchase invoice agree to the purchase order.

This is to ensure that:

- what was ordered was received
- the price charged is that agreed.

Once it is certain that the purchase invoice agrees with the goods that were ordered then the invoice can be authorised for payment.

4.6 Bin cards

The storekeeper must know at any time how much of any item he has in inventory. This is done by use of a bin card.

 Definition

A **bin card** is a simple record of receipts, issues and balances of inventory in hand kept by storekeepers, recorded in quantities of materials inventory.

The bin card is a duplication of the quantity information recorded in the stores ledger (see later in this chapter) but storekeepers frequently find that such a ready record is a very useful aid in carrying out their duties.

An example of a bin card for an item of inventory is given below.

BIN CARD

Description ....*Chipboard*.......... Location......*Stores*......... Code....*D35*....

Maximum *3,000m*. Minimum ...*1,000m*... Reorder level *1,400m* Reorder quantity....*200m*.

	Receipts			Issues			Current inventory level	On order		
Date	GRN ref	Quantity	Issue date	Ref	Quantity		Date	Ref	Quantity
04/7/X3	8737	200m				200m	01/8/ X3	PO6752	300m
30/7/X3	8748	300m				500m			
			07/8/X3	3771	400m	100m			

The bin card does not have value columns.

4.7 Stores ledger account

As well as the information recorded by the storekeeper on a bin card, the accounts department also keep records for each line of inventory, in terms of both quantity and value, and this is known as the stores ledger account.

 Definition

A stores ledger account records the quantity and value of receipts and issues and the current balance of each item of inventory.

The stores ledger account for the item of inventory recorded in the bin card earlier in this section is given below:

STORES LEDGER ACCOUNT

Material Chipboard

Code D35

Date	Receipts				Issues				Balance		
	GRN Ref	Qty	Price per unit £	Amount £	Issue ref	Qty per unit	Price £	Amount £	Qty per unit	Price £	Value £
30/7/X3	8737	200m	2.00	400.00					200	2.00	400.00
06/8/X3	8748	300m	2.00	600.00					500	2.00	1,000.00
07/8/X3					3771	400m	2.00	800.00	100	2.00	200.00

Answers to chapter activities

 Activity 1

Method	Cost of issue on 19 June	Closing inventory at 30 June
FIFO	£2,000	£3,100
LIFO	£2,200	£2,900
AVCO	£2,080	£3,020

Workings

FIFO

- The issue will be made up of all 100 units from June 2, all 200 units from June 3 and 100 of those purchased on June 6 at a price of 1,200/200 = £6 per unit.

- Cost of issue = £400 + £1,000 + (£100 × 6) = £2,000

- Total purchases = £400 + £1,000 + £1,200 + £2,500 = £5,100

- Closing inventory = £5,100 – £2,000 = £3,100

LIFO

- The issue will be made up of all 200 units from June 6 and all 200 units from June 3.

- Cost of issue = £1,200 + £1,000 = £2,200

- Closing inventory = £5,100 – £2,200 = £2,900

AVCO

- Before June 19 we had bought a total of 500 units at a total cost of £400 + £1,000 + £1,200 = £2,600

- On average this works out at £2,600/500 = £5.20 per unit

- Thus the cost of the issue will be 400 × £5.20 = £2,080

- Closing inventory = £5,100 – £2,080 = £3,020

Activity 2

Jetty Ltd has opening inventory of raw material X of 1,500 units at £2 per unit. In the month another 1,000 units at £4.50 are received and the following week 1,800 units are issued.

Identify whether the statements in the table below are true or false by putting a tick in the relevant column.

Statement	True	False
FIFO values the closing inventory at £1,400.		☑
LIFO costs the issue at £6,100.	☑	
AVCO costs the issue at £5,400.	☑	

 Activity 3

Flotsam Ltd has opening inventory of raw material P of 3,000 units at £4.50 per unit. In the month another 2,000 units at £7 are received and the following week 3,750 units are issued.

Identify the valuation method described in the statements below by putting a tick in the relevant column.

Statement	FIFO	LIFO	AVCO
The closing inventory is valued at £6,875			☑
The issue of 3,750 units is costed at £18,750	☑		
The issue of 3,750 units is costed at £21,875		☑	

Activity 4

Characteristic	FIFO	LIFO	AVCO
• Issues are valued at the most recent purchase cost.		☑	
• Inventory is valued at the average of the cost of purchases.			☑
• Inventory is valued at the most recent purchase cost.	☑		

Activity 5

	True	False
• FIFO costs issues of inventory at the most recent purchase price.		☑
• AVCO costs issues of inventory at the oldest purchase price.		☑
• LIFO costs issues of inventory at the oldest purchase price.		☑
• FIFO values closing inventory at the most recent purchase price.	☑	
• LIFO values closing inventory at the most recent purchase price.		☑
• AVCO values closing inventory at the latest purchase price.		☑

Activity 6

Element	Total cost	Unit cost
Materials	£60,000	£4.00
Labour	£75,000	£5.00
Overheads	£60,000	£4.00
Total	£195,000	£13.00

Activity 7

Units	Fixed costs	Variable costs	Total costs	Unit cost
1,000	£60,000	£2,000	£62,000	£62.00
2,000	£60,000	£4,000	£64,000	£32.00
3,000	£60,000	£6,000	£66,000	£22.00
4,000	£60,000	£8,000	£68,000	£17.00

Activity 8

	£
Opening inventory of raw materials	14,000
Purchases of raw materials	60,000
Closing inventory of raw materials	(10,000)
DIRECT MATERIALS USED	64,000
Direct labour	36,000
DIRECT COST	**100,000**
Manufacturing overheads	47,000
MANUFACTURING COST	**147,000**
Opening inventory of work in progress	42,000
Closing inventory of work in progress	(32,000)
COST OF GOODS MANUFACTURED	**157,000**
Opening inventory of finished goods	60,000
Closing inventory of finished goods	(70,000)
COST OF GOODS SOLD	**147,000**

5 Test your knowledge

 Workbook Activity 9

Identify the correct inventory valuation method from the characteristic given by putting a tick in the relevant column of the table below.

Characteristic	FIFO	LIFO	AVCO
• Issues are valued at the most recent purchase cost.			
• Issues are valued at the oldest purchase cost.			
• Issues are valued at the average of the cost of purchases.			
• Inventory is valued at the most recent purchase cost.			
• Inventory is valued at the oldest purchase cost.			

Workbook Activity 10

Adamkus Ltd has the following movements in a certain inventory item into and out of it stores for the month of March:

Date	Receipts		Issues	
	Units	Cost	Units	Cost
March 5	100	£200		
March 12	100	£250		
March 19	200	£600		
March 23			300	
March 27	400	£1,350		

Complete the table below for the issue and closing inventory values.

Method	Cost of issue on 23 March	Closing inventory at 31 March
FIFO		
LIFO		
AVCO		

Workbook Activity 11

Identify the following statements as either true or false.

Statement	True	False
• FIFO costs issues of inventory at the oldest purchase price.		
• AVCO values closing inventory at the oldest purchase price.		
• LIFO costs issues of inventory at the oldest purchase price.		

Workbook Activity 12

Chiluba Ltd is costing a single product with the following cost details:

Variable costs per unit

Materials	£10
Labour	£5
Total fixed costs	£150,000

Complete the following total cost and unit cost table for a production level of 20,000 units.

Element	Total cost	Unit cost
Materials	£	£
Labour	£	£
Overheads	£	£
Total	£	£

 Workbook Activity 13

Complete the table below showing fixed costs, variable costs, total costs and unit cost at the different levels of production.

Units	Fixed costs	Variable costs	Total costs	Unit cost
1,000	£200,000	£5,000	£205,000	£205.00
2,000	£	£	£	£
3,000	£	£	£	£
4,000	£	£	£	£

Workbook Activity 14

Reorder the following costs into a manufacturing account format:

	£
COST OF GOODS MANUFACTURED	**31,400**
MANUFACTURING COST	**29,400**
DIRECT COST	**20,000**
COST OF GOODS SOLD	**29,400**
DIRECT MATERIALS USED	**12,800**
Manufacturing overheads	9,400
Purchases of raw materials	12,000
Opening inventory of raw materials	2,800
Closing inventory of finished goods	(14,000)
Opening inventory of work in progress	8,400
Direct labour	7,200
Closing inventory of raw materials	(2,000)
Closing inventory of work in progress	(6,400)
Opening inventory of finished goods	12,000

Reorder the following costs into a manufacturing account format.

	£
COST OF GOODS MANUFACTURED	31,400
MANUFACTURING COST	29,400
DIRECT COST	20,000
COST OF GOODS SOLD	29,400
DIRECT MATERIALS USED	12,800
Manufacturing overheads	9,400
Purchases of raw materials	12,000
Opening inventory of raw materials	2,800
Closing inventory of finished goods	(14,000)
Opening inventory of work in progress	8,400
Direct labour	7,200
Closing inventory of raw materials	(2,000)
Closing inventory of work in progress	(6,400)
Opening inventory of finished goods	12,000

Labour costs

Introduction

This chapter considers labour costs in more detail.

KNOWLEDGE

1.4 Identify sources of information for historic, current and forecast periods

2.1 Explain how materials, labour and expenses are classified and recorded

SKILLS

2.6 Use these methods to calculate payments for labour: time rate, piecework rate, bonuses

2.8 Calculate the direct cost of a product or service

CONTENTS

1   Introduction
2   Time related pay
3   Output related pay
4   Bonus schemes
5   Sources of information

1 Introduction

1.1 Labour costs

In this unit you need to understand and be able to explain methods of payment for labour to include basic rate (time rate), payment of overtime, payment of bonus and payment by piecework.

You will not be required to have knowledge of specific bonus schemes

1.2 Direct and indirect labour

Just as materials can be classified as direct or indirect so too can labour costs, depending on the job of the employee.

 Example

In a manufacturing organisation the factory workers who make the products would be direct labour whereas the factory supervisor would be an example of an indirect labour cost as although he is working in the factory he is not actually making any of the products.

 Activity 1

Identify the following statements as true or false by putting a tick in the relevant column of the table below.

Cost	True	False
Direct labour costs can be identified with the goods being made or the service being produced.		
Indirect costs vary directly with the level of activity.		

1.3 Calculating gross pay

There are two main methods of calculating the gross pay of employees:

- pay employees for the time spent at work (time related pay)
- pay employees for the work actually produced (output related pay).

In addition there may be bonus schemes to be incorporated. These are covered in more detail later in the chapter.

KAPLAN PUBLISHING

2 Time related pay

2.1 Time related pay

Employees paid under a time related pay method are paid for the hours that they spend at work regardless of the amount of production or output that they achieve in that time. Time related pay employees can be split into two types, **salaried employees** and **hourly rate employees**.

2.2 Salaried employees

 Definition

A **salaried employee** is one whose gross pay is agreed at a fixed amount for a period of time whatever hours that employee works in that period.

This might be expressed as an annual salary such as £18,000 per year or as a weekly rate such as £269.50 per week.

Each organisation will have a set number of hours that are expected to be worked each week, for example a standard working week of 37.5 hours, and salaried employees will be expected to work for at least this number of hours each week.

However if the salaried employee works for more than the standard number of hours for the week then the employment agreement may specify that overtime payments are to be made for the additional hours.

2.3 Hourly rate employees

 Definition

An **hourly rate employee** is one who is paid a set hourly rate for each hour that he works.

These employees are paid for the actual number of hours of attendance in a period, usually a week. A rate of pay will be set for each hour of attendance.

2.4 Overtime

 Definition

Overtime is the number of hours worked by an employee which is greater than the number of hours set by the organisation as the working week.

It is common that employees that work overtime are paid an additional amount per hour for those extra hours.

2.5 Overtime premium

 Definition

Overtime premium is the amount over and above the normal hourly rate that employees are paid for overtime hours.

 Example

An employee's basic week is 40 hours at a rate of pay of £8 per hour. Overtime is paid at 'time and a half'. The employee works a 45-hour week. What is the total gross pay for this employee for the week?

	£
Basic hours 40 × £8	320.00
Overtime 5 × £12	60.00
	───────
	380.00
	───────

The overtime payment can be split between the basic rate element and the overtime premium:

	£
Basic pay 5 × £8	40.00
Overtime premium 5 × £4	20.00
	───────
	60.00

KAPLAN PUBLISHING

Activity 2

Singh Ltd pays a time-rate of £12 per hour to its direct labour for a standard 35 hour week. Any of the labour force working in excess of 35 hours is paid an overtime rate of £15 per hour.

Calculate the gross wage for the week for the workers in the table below.

Worker	Hours worked	Basic wage £	Overtime £	Gross wage £
J. Patel	35			
D. Smith	38			
S. O'Leary	42			

3 Output related pay

Output related pay is also known as 'payment by results' or 'piecework'. This is a direct alternative to time related pay.

 Definition

Payment by results or piecework is where a fixed amount is paid per unit of output achieved irrespective of the time spent.

3.1 Advantages of payment by results

As far as an employee is concerned, payment by results means that they can earn whatever they wish within certain parameters. The harder they work and the more units they produce the higher the wage they will earn.

From the employer's point of view higher production or output can also be encouraged with a system of differential piecework (see later in chapter).

3.2 Problems with payment by results

There are two main problems associated with payment by results. One is the problem of accurate recording of the actual output produced. The amount claimed to be produced determines the amount of pay and, therefore, is potentially open to abuse unless it can be adequately supervised. A system of job sheets and checking of job sheets needs to be in place.

The second problem is that of the maintenance of the quality of the work. If the employee is paid by the amount that is produced then the temptation might be to produce more units but of a lower quality.

For these reasons basic piecework systems are rare in practice – variations of these systems are used instead.

 Activity 3

Stizgt Ltd uses a piecework method to pay labour in one of its factories. The rate used is 90p per unit produced.

Calculate the gross wage for the week for the workers in the table below.

Worker	Units produced in week	Gross wage £
S. McHenry	200 units	
D. Weaver	320 units	
S. Hasina	250 units	

3.3 Piece rate with guarantee

A **piece rate with guarantee** gives the employee some security if the employer does not provide enough work in a particular period. The way that the system works is that if an employee's earnings for the amount of units produced in the period are lower than the guaranteed amount then the guaranteed amount is paid instead.

Activity 4

Fernando is paid £3.00 for every unit that he produces but he has a guaranteed wage of £28.00 per eight hour day. In a particular week he produces the following number of units:

Monday	12 units
Tuesday	14 units
Wednesday	9 units
Thursday	14 units
Friday	8 units

Calculate Fernando's wage for this week.

4 Bonus schemes

Bonuses may be paid to employees for a variety of reasons. An individual employee, a department, a division or the entire organisation may have performed particularly well and it is felt by the management that a bonus is due to some or all of the employees.

4.1 Basic principle of bonuses

The basic principle of a bonus payment is that the employee is rewarded for any additional income or savings in cost to the organisation. This may be, for example, because the employee has managed to save a certain amount of time on the production of a product or a number of products. This time saving will save the organisation money and the amount saved will tend to be split between the organisation and the employee on some agreed basis. The amount paid to the employee/employees is known as the bonus.

4.2 Method of payment

The typical bonus payable will often depend on the method of payment of the employee. The calculation and payment of bonuses will differ for salaried employees, employees paid by results and employees paid on a time rate basis.

Activity 5

Meidani Ltd uses a time-rate method with bonus to pay its direct labour in one of its factories. The time-rate used is £10 per hour and a worker is expected to produce 6 units an hour, anything over this and the worker is paid a bonus of £2 per unit.

Calculate the gross wage for the week for the workers in the table below.

Worker	Hours worked	Units produced	Basic wage £	Bonus £	Gross wage £
J. Klestil	35	220			
C. Zemin	35	205			
J. Chirac	40	240			

 Activity 6

Identify the labour payment method by putting a tick in the relevant column of the table below.

Payment method	Time-rate	Piece-rate	Time-rate plus bonus
Labour is paid based on the production achieved.			
Labour is paid extra if an agreed level of output is exceeded.			
Labour is paid according to hours worked.			

KAPLAN PUBLISHING

Activity 7

Identify one **advantage** for each labour payment method by putting a tick in the relevant column of the table below.

Payment method	Time-rate	Piece-rate	Time-rate plus bonus
Assured level of remuneration for employee.			
Employee earns more if they work more efficiently than expected.			
Assured level of remuneration and reward for working efficiently.			

5 Sources of information

5.1 Documentation and procedures to record labour costs

When an employee joins an organisation it must record details of the employee, their job and pay. This is done by the personnel department in the individual employee's personnel record.

Details that might be kept about an employee are as follows:

- full name, address and date of birth
- personal details such as marital status and emergency contact name and address
- National Insurance number
- previous employment history
- educational details
- professional qualifications
- date of joining organisation
- employee number or code
- clock number issued
- job title and department

- rate of pay agreed

- holiday details agreed

- bank details if salary is to be paid directly into bank account

- amendments to any of the details above (such as increases in agreed rates of pay)

- date of termination of employment (when this takes place) and reasons for leaving.

5.2 Employee record of attendance

On any particular day an employee may be at work, on holiday, absent due to sickness or absent for some other reason. A record must be kept of these details for each day.

This information about an employee's attendance will come from various sources such as clock cards, time sheets, job sheets, and job cards.

6 Summary

In this chapter we looked at different ways of calculating a labour cost. Make sure you can distinguish between time-rate, piece-rate and bonus schemes.

Answers to chapter activities

Activity 1

Cost	True	False
Direct labour costs can be identified with the goods being made or the service being produced.	☑	
Indirect costs vary directly with the level of activity.		☑

Activity 2

Worker	Hours worked	Basic wage £	Overtime £	Gross wage £
J. Patel	35	420	0	420
D. Smith	38	420	45	465
S. O'Leary	42	420	105	525

Activity 3

Worker	Units produced in week	Gross wage £
S. McHenry	200 units	180.00
D. Weaver	320 units	288.00
S. Hasina	250 units	225.00

Activity 4

Fernando would be paid £176.

Working:

Total weekly wage

	£
Monday (12 × 3)	36
Tuesday (14 × 3)	42
Wednesday (guarantee)	28
Thursday (14 × 3)	42
Friday (guarantee)	28
	176

The payment of a guaranteed amount is not a bonus for good work but simply an additional payment required if the amount of production is below a certain level.

Activity 5

Worker	Hours worked	Units produced	Basic wage £	Bonus £	Gross wage £
J. Klestil	35	220	350	20	370
C. Zemin	35	205	350	0	350
J. Chirac	40	240	400	0	400

Working:

- Basic wage = £10 × hours worked

- In 35 hours we would expect 35 × 6 = 210 units.
  J Klestil exceeded this by 10 units, giving a bonus of 10 × 2 = £20
  C. Zemin did not, so received no bonus.

- In 40 hours we would expect 40 × 6 = 240 units.
  J. Chirac did not exceed this, so received no bonus.

KAPLAN PUBLISHING

Activity 6

Payment method	Time-rate	Piece-rate	Time-rate plus bonus
Labour is paid based on the production achieved.		☑	
Labour is paid extra if an agreed level of output is exceeded.			☑
Labour is paid according to hours worked.	☑		

Activity 7

Payment method	Time-rate	Piece-rate	Time-rate plus bonus
Assured level of remuneration for employee.	☑		
Employee earns more if they work more efficiently than expected.		☑	
Assured level of remuneration and reward for working efficiently.			☑

7 Test your knowledge

 Workbook Activity 8

Karimov Ltd pays a time-rate of £10 per hour to its direct labour for a standard 37 hour week. Any of the labour force working in excess of 37 hours is paid 'time and a half'.

Calculate the gross wage for the week for the workers in the table below.

Worker	Hours worked	Basic wage £	Overtime £	Gross wage £
M. Khan	42			
D. Murphy	37			
K. Ng	40			

 Workbook Activity 9

Gibson plc uses a piecework method to pay labour to make clothing in one of its factories. The rate used is £2.50 per garment completed.

Calculate the gross wage for the week for the workers in the table below.

Worker	Units produced in week	Gross wage £
H. Potter	100 units	
T. Riddle	130 units	
S. Snape	175 units	

Workbook Activity 10

Leonid is paid £5.00 for every unit that he produces but he has a guaranteed minimum wage of £25.00 per day.

Calculate Leonid's wage for this week by filling in the following table:

Day	Units produced	Gross wage £
Monday	4 units	
Tuesday	6 units	
Wednesday	9 units	
Thursday	3 units	
Friday	8 units	
Total	30 units	

 Workbook Activity 11

Legolas Ltd uses a time-rate method with bonus to pay its direct labour in one of its factories. The time-rate used is £12 per hour and a worker is expected to produce 10 units an hour, anything over this and the worker is paid a bonus of £1 per unit.

Calculate the gross wage for the week for the workers in the table below.

Worker	Hours worked	Units produced	Basic wage £	Bonus £	Gross wage £
L. Aragon	37	375			
T. Ent	35	360			
K. Theodin	42	410			

Budgeting

5

Introduction

This chapter looks briefly at budgeting before focussing on variances and how they can be used to help control an organisation.

SKILLS
3.3 Enter budgeted and actual data on income and expenditure into a spreadsheet to provide a comparison of the results and identify differences

CONTENTS
1 Budgeting
2 Identifying budgeted costs
3 Variances

1 Budgeting

1.1 Introduction

In this unit you need to have a brief knowledge of budgeting as an aid to planning and control but this need only be at a basic level.

You will not be required to explain the nature of budgeted costs in any great detail, but will be required to identify budgeted costs and to compare with actual costs by using variances.

1.2 What is budgeting?

Budgets set out the costs and revenues that are expected to be incurred or earned in future periods.

For example, if you are planning to take a holiday, you will probably have a budgeted amount that you can spend. This budget will determine where you go and for how long.

Most organisations prepare budgets for the business as a whole. The following budgets may also be prepared by organisations:

- Departmental budgets.

- Functional budgets (for sales, production, expenditure and so on).

- Statements of profit or loss/income statements (in order to determine the expected future profits).

- Cash budgets (in order to determine future cash flows).

1.3 Budgetary control

As stated in chapter 1, the main reason for budgeting is to help managers control the business.

The budget contains a mixture of what you think will happen and what you intend to make happen.

For example, suppose we think we will be able to sell 100 units in June (a sales forecast) and therefore plan to make 100 units in May (a production budget). This means we need to buy 200 kg of material X at an expected cost of £5 per kg (a materials purchases budget)

This then gives a benchmark against which we can evaluate actual performance.

For example, what if we only sold 90 units, or used 210 kg of material or it cost £5.50/kg not £5.

Any difference or 'variance' can then be investigated to identify the cause. Once we know this we can take appropriate action.

For example, if the price of materials was higher because our normal supplier put their prices up, then we could consider trying to find another supplier.

1.4 Other reasons for budgeting

Other reasons for budgeting include the following:

- **Authorisation**

  A budget may act as a formal authorisation to a manager to spend a given amount on specified activities.

- **Forecasting**

  Forecasting refers to the prediction of events over which little or no control is exercised. Some parts of all budgets are, therefore, based on forecasts.

- **Planning**

  Planning is an attempt to shape the future by a conscious effort to influence those factors which are open to control.

- **Communication and co-ordination**

  Budgets communicate plans to managers responsible for carrying them out. They also ensure co-ordination between managers of sub-units so that each is aware of the others' requirements.

- **Motivation**

  Budgets are often intended to motivate managers to perform in line with organisational plans and objectives.

- **Evaluation**

  The performance of managers and organisational units is often evaluated by reference to budgetary targets.

2 Identifying budgeted costs

2.1 Introduction

Within the basic costing unit you will need to be able to calculate total and unit costs at different activity levels.

2.2 Cost behaviour

When calculating budgeted costs remember to distinguish between variable costs and fixed costs

- Fixed costs will remain constant for each activity level.

- Variable costs will increase in line with activity levels.

Example

Complete the table below showing budgeted fixed costs, variable costs, total costs and unit cost at the different possible budgeted levels of production

Units	Fixed costs	Variable costs	Total costs	Unit cost
100	400	200	600	6.00
200				
300				

Solution

Units	Fixed costs	Variable costs	Total costs	Unit cost
100	400	200	600	6.00
200	400	400	800	4.00
300	400	600	1,000	3.33

Notes: You may recall doing similar calculations in chapter 1

- Fixed costs do not change

- To get variable costs either

  (a) simply prorate – e.g. to go from 100 to 300 units the volume has trebled , so treble the cost: 3 × 200 = £600, or

  (b) first calculate the variable cost per unit = 200/100 = £2 per unit. This can be used to work out other variable costs, so for 300 units the variable cost will be 300 × 2 = £600.

- Total costs are simply the sum of fixed and variable.

- To get the unit cost, divide the total cost by the number of units. So for 200 units the unit cost = £800/200 = £4 per unit.

 Activity 1

Complete the table below showing budgeted fixed costs, variable costs, total costs and unit cost at the different budgeted levels of production.

Units	Fixed costs	Variable costs	Total costs	Expected unit cost
1,000	£2,400	£600	£3,000	£3.00
2,000				
3,000				
4,000				

Activity 2

Moussa Ltd is budgeting for the costs of a single product which has the following cost details:

Variable costs per unit

- Materials £5 per unit
- Labour £8 per unit

Total fixed costs £60,000

Complete the following budgeted total cost and unit cost table for a production level of 30,000 units.

Element	Total cost £	Unit cost £
Materials		
Labour		
Overheads		
Total		

 Activity 3

Barak Ltd makes a single product and has estimated the following expected costs for a budgeted production level of 12,000 units:

- Materials 3,600 kg at £5 per kg
- Labour 600 hours at £12 per hour
- Overheads £60,000

Complete the table below to show the expected unit cost at the production level of 12,000 units.

Element	Unit cost £
Materials	
Labour	
Overheads	
Total	

3 Variances

3.1 What is a variance?

The difference between actual and expected (or budgeted) cost is known as a variance.

- A **favourable** variance ("Fav") is when the actual cost is lower than expected and

- An **adverse** variance ("Adv") is when actual cost is higher than expected.

3.2 How to calculate a variance

For Basic Costing the only calculations required will be a comparison of actual to expected costs or revenues.

 Example

Fujimori Ltd has produced a performance report detailing budgeted and actual material cost for last month.

Calculate the amount of the variance and then determine whether it is adverse or favourable by putting a tick in the relevant column of the table below.

Cost type	Budget £	Actual £	Variance £	Adv.	Fav.
Materials	24,500	26,200			

Solution

Cost type	Budget £	Actual £	Variance £	Adv.	Fav.
Materials	24,500	26,200	1,700	☑	

Notes:

- Variance = 26,200 – 24,500 = £1,700

- The variance is adverse as **the actual cost is higher** than budgeted

Example 3

Sushi Ltd has produced a performance report detailing budgeted and actual sales revenue for last year.

Calculate the amount of the variance and then determine whether it is adverse or favourable by putting a tick in the relevant column of the table below.

Cost type	Budget £	Actual £	Variance £	Adv.	Fav.
Sales	17,500	16,950			

Solution

Cost type	Budget £	Actual £	Variance £	Adv.	Fav.
Sales	17,500	16,950	550	☑	

Notes:

- Variance = £17,500 – £16,950 = £550

- The variance is adverse as the **actual revenue is lower** than budgeted.

 Activity 4

Kagame Ltd has produced a performance report detailing budgeted and actual cost for last month.

Calculate the amount of the variance for each cost type and then determine whether it is adverse or favourable by putting a tick in the relevant column of the table below.

Cost type	Budget £	Actual £	Variance £	Adv.	Fav.
Materials	56,000	49,500			
Labour	64,000	65,200			
Overheads	150,000	148,500			

Activity 5

Identify the following statements as being true or false by putting a tick in the relevant column of the table below.

Statement	True	False
A variance is the difference between budgeted and actual cost.		
A favourable variance means budgeted costs are greater than actual costs.		
An adverse variance means you have made a saving compared to budgeted costs.		

3.3 Evaluating the significance of a variance

Management do not want to waste time investigating small variances, so will set criteria for deciding what makes a variance large enough to report and investigate.

For example

- "Only investigate variances bigger than £500"

- "Only investigate variances bigger that 5% of budget"

If using a percentage measure then the amount of the variance that exceeds the cut-off percentage is known as the "discrepancy".

 Example

Antrobus Ltd has produced a performance report detailing budgeted and actual material cost for last month. Any variance in excess of 10% of budget is deemed to be significant and should be reviewed.

Calculate the amount of the variance and then determine whether it is significant by putting a tick in the relevant column of the table below.

Cost type	Budget £	Actual £	Variance £	Significant	Not significant
Labour	5,600	5,200			

Solution

Cost type	Budget £	Actual £	Variance £	Significant	Not significant
Labour	5,600	5,200	400		☑

Notes:

- Variance = £5,200 – £5,600 = £400
- As a % of budget this gives (400/5,600) × 100% = 7.1%, which is less than 10%, so the variance is deemed not significant.

 Activity 6

Guterres Ltd has produced a performance report detailing budgeted and actual cost for this month. Any variance in excess of 5% of budget is deemed to be significant and should be reported to the relevant manager.

Examine the variances in the table below and indicate whether they are significant or not by putting a tick in the relevant column.

Cost type	Budget £	Variance £	Significant	Not significant
Direct materials	26,000	1,200		
Direct labour	35,000	2,000		
Production overheads	15,000	1,100		
Selling costs	2,000	90		

 Summary

In this chapter we looked briefly at budgeting, how to calculate budget costs and the basics of variance analysis.

Answers to chapter activities

Activity 1

Units	Fixed costs	Variable costs	Total costs	Unit cost
1,000	£2,400	£600	£3,000	£3.00
2,000	£2,400	£1,200	£3,600	£1.80
3,000	£2,400	£1,800	£4,200	£1.40
4,000	£2,400	£2,400	£4,800	£1.20

Activity 2

Element	Total cost £	Unit cost £
Materials	150,000	5
Labour	240,000	8
Overheads	60,000	2
Total	450,000	15

Activity 3

Element	Unit cost £
Materials	1.50
Labour	0.60
Overheads	5.00
Total	7.10

Notes:

- To get material costs per unit, either

  (a) calculate the total material cost (3,600 × £5 = 18,000) and divide this by the number of units: 18,000 ÷ 12,000 = £1.50 per unit, or

  (b) first calculate the usage per unit = 3,600/12,000 = 0.3 kg per unit. The cost per unit is then 0.3 kg at £5 per kg = £1.50.

- To get labour costs per unit, either

  (a) calculate the total labour cost (600 × £12=£7,200) and divide this by the number of units: £7,200 ÷ 12,000 = £0.60 per unit, or

  (b) first calculate the time per unit = 600/12,000 = 0.05 hours per unit. The cost per unit is then 0.05 hours at £12 per hour = £0.60.

- To get the overhead unit cost, divide the total cost by the number of units = £60,000/12,000 = £5 per unit

Activity 4

Cost type	Budget £	Actual £	Variance £	Adv.	Fav.
Materials	56,000	49,500	6,500		☑
Labour	64,000	65,200	1,200	☑	
Overheads	150,000	148,500	1,500		☑

Activity 5

Statement	True	False
A variance is the difference between budgeted and actual cost.	☑	
A favourable variance means budgeted costs are greater than actual costs.	☑	
An adverse variance means you have made a saving compared to budgeted costs.		☑

Activity 6

Cost type	Budget £	Variance £	Significant	Not significant
Direct materials	26,000	1,200		☑
Direct Labour	35,000	2,000	☑	
Production overheads	15,000	1,100	☑	
Selling costs	2,000	90		☑

Workings

- Materials   (1,200/26,000) × 100   = 4.6%
- Labour   (2,000/35,000) × 100   = 5.7%
- Overheads   (1,100/15,000) × 100   = 7.3%
- Selling costs   (90/2,000) × 100   = 4.5%

5 Test your knowledge

 Workbook Activity 7

Ben Ali Ltd has produced a performance report detailing budgeted and actual cost for last month.

Calculate the amount of the variance for each cost type and then determine whether it is adverse or favourable by putting a tick in the relevant column of the table below.

Cost type	Budget £	Actual £	Variance £	Adv.	Fav.
Sales	175,000	176,850			
Labour	15,000	14,950			
Overheads	120,600	120,000			

 Workbook Activity 8

Identify the following statements as being true or false by putting a tick in the relevant column of the table below.

Statement	True	False
A variance is the difference between actual and budgeted cost.		
A variance is the average of actual and budgeted cost.		
A favourable variance means this cost element would reduce profit compared to budget.		
An adverse variance means you have made a saving compared to budgeted costs.		

Workbook Activity 9

Ionatana Ltd has produced a performance report detailing budgeted and actual material cost for last month. Any variance in excess of 6% of budget is deemed to be significant and should be reviewed.

Calculate the amount of the variance and then determine whether it is significant by putting a tick in the relevant column of the table below.

Cost type	Budget	Actual	Variance	Significant?	
	£	£	£	Yes	No
Direct labour	10,000	9,500			
Direct materials	13,000	15,200			
Production overheads	24,000	25,120			
Administration costs	35,000	32,400			
Selling and distribution costs	45,000	49,260			

Spreadsheets

Introduction

This chapter looks at spreadsheets, their use in business and some of the functions and formulas that spreadsheets use.

KNOWLEDGE

3.2 Explain how spreadsheets can be used to present information on income and expenditure and to facilitate internal reporting.

SKILLS

3.1 Enter income and expenditure data into a spreadsheet.

3.3 Enter budgeted and actual data on income and expenditure into a spreadsheet to provide a comparison of the results and identify differences.

3.4 Use basic spreadsheet functions and formulas.

3.5 Format the spreadsheet to present data in a clear and unambiguous manner and in accordance with operational requirements.

CONTENTS

1   What are spreadsheets?
2   Basic formulas
3   Other functions
4   Uses of spreadsheets

1 What are spreadsheets?

1.1 Definition

A spreadsheet is a computer program that allows numbers to be entered and manipulated. The numbers can be labelled with text to help indicate their meaning. In addition, the numbers can be turned into graphs and charts to help analyse them in more detail.

Essentially, a spreadsheet is a huge table of rows and columns, with columns given letters (A to Z followed by AA to AZ and so on) and rows numbered sequentially from 1 to 65536. Columns and rows are marked by vertical and horizontal lines, so a blank spreadsheet looks like a large table of empty boxes. Each box or 'cell' has a unique identification reference (e.g. cell D7 is in column D and row 7).

A spreadsheet is therefore like a giant calculator. A large amount of information can be entered into the cells.

Each cell may contain:

- Text
- Numbers
- Formulas.

1.2 The parts of a spreadsheet

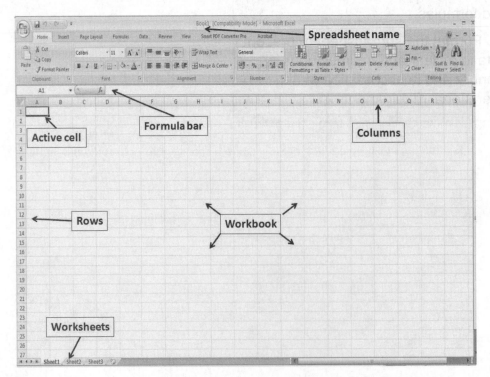

As you can see, the spreadsheet is made up of a number of different parts. The main ones that you need to be aware of are labelled.

- **Workbook**

    This refers to the spreadsheet file itself. The spreadsheet shown above, in its entirety, is known as a workbook.

- **Spreadsheet name**

    This is the name for your workbook. You can call it anything you like. The default name is typically 'Book1' as you can see in the diagram above.

- **Worksheets**

    A worksheet is a single page or sheet in a workbook. By default workbooks are split into three worksheets when you first open them, but you can add as many more as you like. You can move between worksheets simply by clicking on them – just like turning a page in a book.

- **Active cell**

    This is the cell that you are currently working in. It is highlighted with a bold border. The row number and column number of the cell are both highlighted as well. As you can see in the above diagram, the active cell is at the junction of column A and row 1, meaning that the active cell is A1. You can enter data into the active cell. The active cell can be changed by clicking on a different cell.

- **Formula bar**

    This displays the data or formula stored in the active cell. You can use it to input or amend information in the cell.

1.3 Entering data into a spreadsheet

As mentioned in section 1.2, data can be entered into the active cell. We click on the cell we wish to add information to and then enter the data.

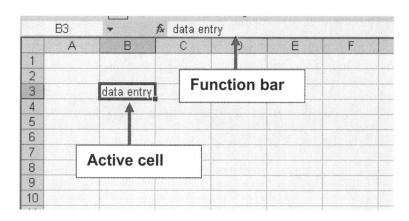

The data can be entered into the cell in one of two different places. It can be typed directly into the active cell itself or into the formula bar.

 Example

Fry Ltd makes a single product and has the following income and expenditure information:

Sales revenue: £7 per unit

Variable costs: £2 per unit

Fixed costs: £7,000 per week

The number of units sold by Fry during the last three weeks has been as follows:

Week one: 1,500 units

Week two: 2,000 units

Week three: 2,400 units

Complete the formatting of the spreadsheet by identifying which of the following column headings should be placed in each cell marked with '?':

Total costs

Profit/(loss)

Fixed costs

Complete the rows for week 2 and week 3 by inserting figures in the cells.

	A	B	C	D	E	F
1		?	Variable costs	?	Sales revenue	?
2	Week 1	7,000	3,000	10,000	10,500	500
3	Week 2					
4	Week 3					

Solution:

	A	B	C	D	E	F
1		Fixed costs	Variable costs	Total costs	Sales revenue	Profit/(loss)
2	Week 1	7,000	3,000	10,000	10,500	500
3	Week 2	7,000	4,000	11,000	14,000	3,000
4	Week 3	7,000	4,800	11,800	16,800	5,000

Notes:

To decide on the column headings, look at the information you have been given in the row for week 1. We can see that cell B2 has 7,000 as its value – indicating that these must be the fixed costs, which are 7,000 each week. Add this to the variable costs and we get 10,000 – the figure in cell D2. Column D must therefore be total costs. The value column F is the difference between sales revenue and total costs, so this must represent the profit or loss for the period.

Once you've decided on what goes into each column, you need to fill in the rest of the table for the following weeks. This is a similar exercise to the examples we saw in Chapter 5 – this time we are putting the information into the cells of a spreadsheet.

 Activity 1

Leela Ltd makes a single product and has the following income and expenditure information:

Sales revenue: £25 per unit

Variable costs: £15 per unit

Fixed costs: £18,000 per week

The number of units sold by Leela during the last three months has been as follows:

January: 2,100 units

February: 1,700 units

March: 2,600 units

> **Complete the formatting of the spreadsheet by identifying which of the following column headings should be placed in each cell marked with '?':**
>
> Sales revenue
>
> Profit/(loss)
>
> Variable costs
>
> **Complete the rows for February and March by inserting figures in the cells.**

	A	B	C	D	F
1		?	Fixed costs	?	?
2	January	52,500	18,000	31,500	3,000
3	February				
4	March				

2 Basic formulas

2.1 Introduction

In the examples we have seen so far, we have had to calculate our own profit or loss figures using a calculator and then place the correct figure into the appropriate cell in the spreadsheet.

In the real world, performing calculations like this manually before inputting them into the spreadsheet would be extremely time consuming. Most spreadsheets therefore have a number of formulas that can be inputted into the cells that will undertake key calculations automatically for you.

There are many different formulas within spreadsheet programs, but for our purposes there are five key formulas that you need to be able to use:

- Add
- Total
- Subtract
- Multiply
- Divide.

All formulas have to start with an equals sign (=) otherwise the spreadsheet will not know what you are doing and will treat your entry as text.

2.2 Add

Let's say that you have inputted a set of figures into your spreadsheet as follows:

We have listed our sales but we need to calculate the total of all the sales we have made so far and place it into cell C9.

One way of doing this is to use the 'add' formula. To do this, type in the cell references of the numbers you want to add together, with the symbol '+' between them. Don't forget to start the formula with an '='.

For our spreadsheet, the formula would therefore need to be:

=C3+C4+C5+C6+C7

We would then press the 'enter' button on the keyboard and the total of 31,800 will be displayed in cell C9.

2.3 Total (sum)

One problem with the 'add' function is that it can mean creating a rather long formula if there are lots of cells you need to add together (as you can see above). The 'sum' function can help with this problem by letting you add up an entire row or column of figures quickly and easily.

To add up the figures from our diagram above using the sum function, find the cell references of the beginning and end of the column or row you want to total – in this case we want to add the column from cells C3 to C7.

The formula we would have to enter into cell C9 would therefore be:

=sum(C3:C7)

Again, we would then press the 'enter' button on the keyboard and the total of 31,800 will be displayed in cell C9.

Example

Farnsworth has created the following spreadsheet for his employee's wages in the last month.

	A	B	C
1		Hours	Total pay (£)
2	Zoidberg	148	2,146
3	Wong	120	1,020
4	Rodriguez	128	1,408
5	Total		

Insert the formulas in the table below that should be used in row 5 of columns B and C.

	A	B	C
5	Total		

Solution:

There are two possible ways of answering this question. The first would be to use the 'add' function. To use this, we would add all the cells together from the column above.

	A	B	C
5	Total	=B2+B3+B4	=C2+C3+C4

The alternative would be to use the 'sum' function. This would sum the entire column between the cells specified in the formula.

	A	B	C
5	Total	=sum(B2:B4)	=sum(C2:C4)

You will see from our last example that the 'sum' and 'add' formulas could both be used to calculate a total in a spreadsheet. In your examination, either approach will be acceptable.

Activity 2

Conrad has created a spreadsheet to keep track of his costs.

	A	B	C	D	E
1		April	May	June	Total:
2	Variable costs	15,000	20,000	17,000	
3	Fixed costs	11,000	11,000	11,000	

Insert the formulas into the table below that should be used in cells E2 and E3.

	E
1	Total:
2	
3	

2.4 Subtract

If we need to take one cell from another, we follow the same approach as for addition, but we place a minus (-) sign between the references of the cells in question.

Consider the following spreadsheet:

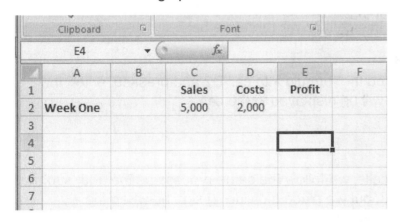

To find the profit figure to be placed in cell E2, we will need to subtract the costs from the sales figure.

The formula to enter into cell E2 will therefore be:

=C2-D2

When we have entered the formula into cell E2 and pressed 'enter' the profit of 3,000 will be displayed in the cell.

2.5   Multiply

If we need to multiply cells together, we follow the same process as the add and subtract formulas, but we place a multiply (*) sign between the references of the cells in question. On most keyboards, this sign is created by pressing the shift and number 8 button at the same time.

Consider the following spreadsheet:

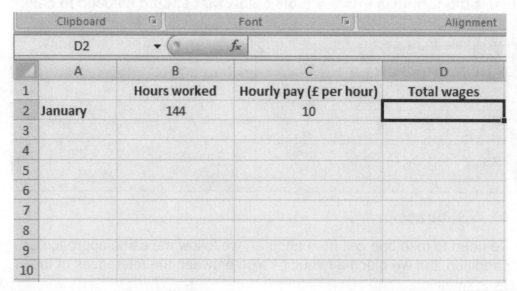

We need to multiply the figures in cell B2 and C2 together to get the total wages figure for cell D2.

The formula to enter into cell D2 will therefore be:

=B2*C2

When we have entered the formula into cell D2 and pressed 'enter' the total wages of 1,440 will be displayed in the cell.

2.6   Divide

If we need to divide cells, we follow the same process as the add, subtract and multiply formulas, but we place a divide (/) sign between the references of the cells in question.

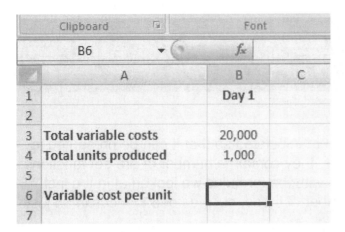

In the spreadsheet above, we want to find the variable cost per unit. To do this, we will need to divide the total variable cost by the total number of units produced in the day.

The formula to be entered into cell B6 would therefore need to be:

=B3/B4

When we have entered the formula into cell B6 and pressed 'enter' the variable cost per unit of 20 will be displayed in the cell.

Activity 3

Robot plc has created a spreadsheet to help calculate details about its income and costs for the year.

	A	B	C	D
		Units	Per unit (£)	Total (£)
1				
2	Sales	2,000	20	
3	Materials	2,000		45,000
4	Labour	2,000	15	
5	Profit			

Enter the formulas that would be required in cells D2, C3, D4 and D5 to complete the spreadsheet.

Note: formulas are NOT required for cells B5 or C5

3 Other functions

3.1 Introduction

Spreadsheets allow data to be manipulated so that it can be presented in various ways. To help with this, they contain a number of pre-set functions that can help you with this. As with the formulas we looked at in the last section, there are a large number of these, but we need to focus in on just three:

- ascending and descending order
- autosum
- average
- express as a percentage.

3.2 Ascending and descending order

Consider a class of ten students who have all taken an exam. Their marks have been placed into a spreadsheet in no particular order.

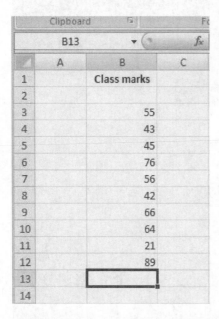

The problem with the marks being shown in this format is that they are hard to interpret. It will take time to identify the top mark in the class and how many passed or failed as you have to read through all the results.

That is where the ascending or descending function becomes useful. To use it, begin by highlighting all of the results in the list. We can them place them in ascending order (i.e. lowest result first, down to the highest at the bottom) or descending order (i.e. highest result first, down to the lowest at the bottom) by pressing the relevant function button.

The function buttons on a spreadsheet typically look like this:

A↓ Sort A to Z
Z↓ Sort Z to A

'A to Z' will give you an ascending order, while 'Z to A' will give you an descending order. To help you remember this, think of Z as always representing the biggest number and A representing the smallest number in the list.

Here is our earlier spreadsheet of student marks, organised both ways:

	Clipboard		Font	
	C13			fx
	A	B	C	
1		**Ascending order:**	**Descending order**	
2		(A to Z)	(Z to A)	
3		21	89	
4		42	76	
5		43	66	
6		45	64	
7		55	56	
8		56	55	
9		64	45	
10		66	43	
11		76	42	
12		89	21	
13				
14				

This is now much easier to interpret – in each case we can quickly and easily see the range of results and identify the highest and lowest figures.

Activity 4

Hermes has created a spreadsheet to keep track of the costs that he incurred on four jobs (numbered 1 to 4) he worked on in the month.

	A	B
1	**Job**	**Costs** (£)
2	Job 1	5,134
3	Job 2	7,443
4	Job 3	9,122
5	Job 4	5,132

Reorder the costs into ascending order. After you have sorted the costs correctly, select from the list the cost that appears in cell B4.

A   7,443

B   5,132

C   9,122

D   5,134

3.3   Autosum

This function gives us an easy way of using the 'sum' function we discussed in the last section by automatically adding up the figures in a number of cells.

The function button for autosum on a spreadsheet would typically look like this:

Note that in the exam they may use the word 'sum' rather than 'autosum' on the function button.

Using our list of class results from earlier – if we wish to add up all the results to get a total mark, we can do this by highlighting the cells with the student marks and then pressing the auto sum button.

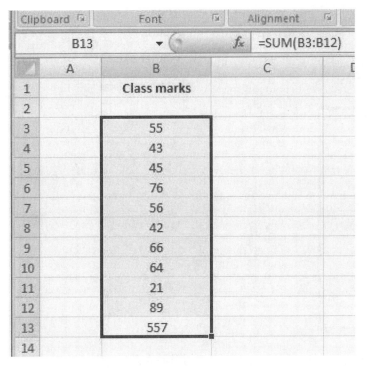

You will notice that this has put the total of the numbers - 557 - highlighted into a cell directly underneath the list (cell B13). As you can see from the function bar, it has done this by automatically creating a sum formula, as we were looking at in the last section of this chapter.

3.4   Average

Another function within the spreadsheet is the ability to automatically work out an average.

For instance, using our list of student results from above, we may wish to know what the average mark was that our students scored.

As with autosum, to calculate this we highlight the cells containing the data that we wish to find the average for.

We then click on the 'average' function button, which typically looks something like this:

Our student spreadsheet would then look something like this (see over):

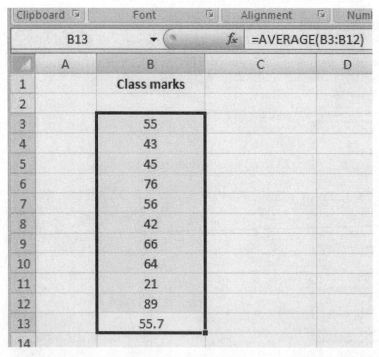

As with autosum, the spreadsheet has calculated the average of the marks and placed it in a cell directly underneath the list (cell B13). It has done this by automatically creating an appropriate formula to help it calculate the average, which you can see in the function bar at the top of the diagram.

3.5 Express as a percentage

Our last key function allows you to express figures as a percentage.

The function button typically looks like this:

Consider this spreadsheet – where we have used a spreadsheet to try and work out variances as a percentage of budget results.

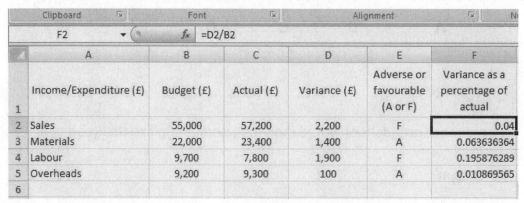

The percentages have been calculated (as you can see from the function bar) by simply dividing the variance cell by the budget cell. This has given the percentage in decimal terms. However, this is not particularly easy to read or well formatted.

Highlighting the cells in column F and pressing the percentage function key restates the cells as percentages which are easier to interpret, as you can see below.

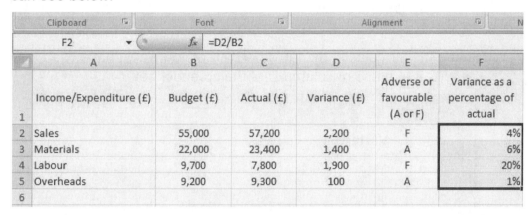

F2	fx =D2/B2				
	A	B	C	D	E	F
1	Income/Expenditure (£)	Budget (£)	Actual (£)	Variance (£)	Adverse or favourable (A or F)	Variance as a percentage of actual
2	Sales	55,000	57,200	2,200	F	4%
3	Materials	22,000	23,400	1,400	A	6%
4	Labour	9,700	7,800	1,900	F	20%
5	Overheads	9,200	9,300	100	A	1%
6						

Note that you can be asked to use your knowledge of spreadsheets in the exam to help you complete variance tables like these in the exam. These questions will be similar to those you saw in Chapter 5.

Activity 5

Scruffy Ltd has partly prepared a spreadsheet to help him calculate his variances for the year. He has filled in his actual and budget results, but has not managed to get any further.

(a) Fill in the remainder of the spreadsheet. Place an A or F in the appropriate cells in column E to indicate whether the variance is adverse or favourable. Quote percentages to the nearest whole percentage.

	A	B	C	D	E	F
1		Budget	Actual	Variance	Adv or Fav	Variance as % of budget
2	Sales	12,000	11,480			
3	Materials	4,000	4,590			
4	Labour	3,500	3,400			
5	Overheads	2,700	2,950			

(b) If Scruffy's policy is to investigate variances over 10% of budget, which of the items of income and expenditure would Scruffy need to investigate?

A   Sales

B   Materials

C   Labour

D   Overheads

(c) Insert the formulas in the table below that you would have used for cells 2, 3, 4 and 5 of column D of the spreadsheet.

	D
1	**Variance**
2	
3	
4	
5	

4   Uses of spreadsheets

Now that we have examined how spreadsheets work, you should be able to identify a number of key uses of spreadsheets. Amongst other things, they can be used to:

- Prepare financial or cash flow forecasts.

- Prepare budgets and other plans.

- Produce reports comparing actual reports with the budget.

- Prepare a statement of profit or loss (income statement) and statement of financial position.

For additional security, spreadsheets can be password protected to ensure that only authorised people can access the data it contains.

Activity 6

Below are four statements about spreadsheets.

Identify the following statements as being true or false by putting a tick in the relevant column of the table below.

Statement	True	False
A worksheet refers to the entire spreadsheet file.		
Spreadsheets cannot be protected through the use of passwords.		
Data is entered into the active cell in the spreadsheet.		
Spreadsheets allow data to be presented in a number of different ways, including graphically.		

5 Summary

In this chapter, we have examined what spreadsheets are and how they can be used. We have also looked at several key functions and formulas that can be used in spreadsheets to help organise and interpret the data that has been entered into them.

Answers to chapter activities

 Activity 1

	A	B	C	D	F
1		**Sales revenue**	Fixed costs	**Variable costs**	**Profit/(loss)**
2	January	52,500	18,000	31,500	3,000
3	February	**42,500**	**18,000**	**25,500**	**(1,000)**
4	March	**65,000**	**18,000**	**39,000**	**8,000**

 Activity 2

Two possible answers would have been acceptable here:

Add function

	E
1	**Total:**
2	=B2+C2+D2
3	=B3+C3+D3

Sum function

	E
1	**Total:**
2	=sum(B2:D2)
3	=sum(B3:D3)

KAPLAN PUBLISHING

Activity 3

Cell D2: =B2*C2

Cell C3: =D3/B3

Cell D4: =B4*C4

Cell D5: =D2-D3-D4

Activity 4

The costs need to be placed into ascending order (A to Z) – so the figures need to run from the lowest to the highest.

This would give us:

B
Costs (£)
5,132
5,134
7,443
9,122

Cell B4 therefore contains 7,443 – which gives us answer A.

Activity 5

(a)

	A	B	C	D	E	F
1		Budget	Actual	Variance	Adv or Fav	Variance as % of budget
2	Sales	12,000	11,480	520	A	4%
3	Materials	4,000	4,590	590	A	15%
4	Labour	3,500	3,400	100	F	3%
5	Overheads	2,700	2,950	250	A	9%

(b)   The company would therefore only investigate materials, giving an answer of B.

(c)   The most appropriate formulas would have been:

	D
1	Variance
2	=B2-C2
3	=B3-C3
4	=B4-C4
5	=B5-C5

Activity 6

Statement	True	False
A worksheet refers to the entire spreadsheet file.		☑
Spreadsheets cannot be protected through the use of passwords.		☑
Data is entered into the active cell in the spreadsheet.	☑	
Spreadsheets allow data to be presented in a number of different ways, including graphically.	☑	

6 Test your knowledge

 Workbook Activity 7

Listed below are four statements about spreadsheets.

Identify the statements as being true or false by putting a tick in the relevant column of the table below.

Statement	True	False
Spreadsheets will not allow data entered into the cells to be rearranged.		
If a password is used, it must also be the title of the spreadsheet.		
A formula tells the spreadsheet to undertake a particular action or calculation.		
Worksheets refer to the different pages of the spreadsheet.		

Workbook Activity 8

Roberto has created a spreadsheet to monitor his staff's wages.

	A	B
1	**Staff member**	**Wages £**
2	Hubert	201
3	Brannigan	176
4	Kiff	195
5	Phillip	177

Reorder the costs into descending order. After you have sorted the variances correctly, select from the list the cost that appears in cell B3.

A   177

B   176

C   201

D   195

Workbook Activity 9

MOMCORP Inc has partly prepared a spreadsheet to help calculate its variances for the year. It only wishes to investigate variances if they are greater than 7% of budget.

(a)   Fill in the remainder of the spreadsheet. Place an A or F in the appropriate cells in column E to indicate whether the variance is adverse or favourable. Place an S or NS in column F to indicate whether the variance is significant or not significant.

	A	B	C	D	E	F
1		Budget	Actual	Variance	Adv or Fav	Significant (S) or Not significant (NS)
2	Sales	1,500	1,670			
3	Materials	895	997			
4	Labour	450	403			
5	Overheads	315	295			

(b)   Insert the formulas in the table below that you would have used for cells 2, 3, 4 and 5 of column D of the spreadsheet.

	D
1	Variance
2	
3	
4	
5	

WORKBOOK ACTIVITIES
ANSWERS

Workbook Activities Answers

1   Cost classification

Workbook Activity 11

Characteristic	Financial accounting	Management accounting
Content can include forecasts.		☑
Looks mainly at historical information.	☑	
Format must conform to statute and accounting standards.	☑	
Any format that seems useful can be used.		☑
Mainly produced to help managers run and control the business.		☑
Would be used by potential investors thinking of buying shares.	☑	
Produced for shareholders.	☑	

Workbook Activity 12

Cost	Production	Admin	Distribution
Purchases of wood to make chairs.	☑		
Depreciation of delivery vans.			☑
HR director's bonus.		☑	
Salaries of production workers.	☑		
Electricity bill for workshop.	☑		
Insurance of sales team laptops.			☑

Workbook Activity 13

Cost	Direct	Indirect
Travelling costs for when staff visit clients.	☑	
Rechargeable accountants' time.	☑	
Office heating costs.		☑
Recruitment costs.		☑
Accountants' time recorded as "general admin." on time sheets.		☑

Workbook Activity 14

Cost	Fixed	Variable	Semi-variable
Sales staff pay.			☑
Motor oil used in servicing.		☑	
Depreciation of premises.	☑		
Mechanics' pay (salaried).	☑		
Electricity.			☑

2   Coding of costs and income

Workbook Activity 4

Product	Code
Boys shoes, brown leather uppers, rubber soles, size 4.	3314240
Ladies slippers, green suede uppers, rubber soles, size 4½.	2653245
Girls shoes, burgundy leather uppers, leather soles, size 3½.	4364135

(i)   Boys shoes, brown leather uppers, rubber soles, size 4.

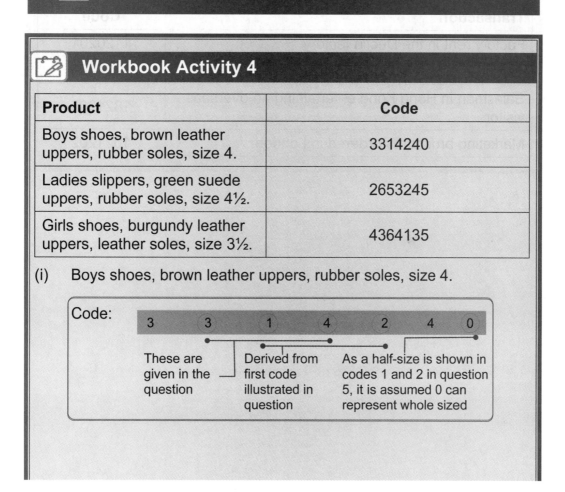

Code:

3   3   1   4   2   4   0

These are given in the question

Derived from first code illustrated in question

As a half-size is shown in codes 1 and 2 in question 5, it is assumed 0 can represent whole sized

(ii)   Ladies slippers, green suede uppers, rubber soles, size 4½.

Code   2   6   5   3   2   4   5

Derived from first code illustrated in question

This was given in the question

As shown in code 1 and 2 in the question

(iii)   Girls shoes, burgundy leather uppers, leather soles, size 3½.

Code   4   3   6   4   1   3   5

Derived from second code in question

Workbook Activity 5

Transaction	Code
Factory rent in the Dublin factory.	1120201
Administration telephone costs incurred in Lagos.	1224203
Salesman in Hong Kong entertaining an overseas visitor.	1821205
Marketing brochures ordered in London.	1021202

KAPLAN PUBLISHING

3 Materials and inventory

Workbook Activity 9

Identify the correct stock valuation method from the characteristic given by putting a tick in the relevant column of the table below.

Characteristic	FIFO	LIFO	AVCO
• Issues are valued at the most recent purchase cost.		☑	
• Issues are valued at the oldest purchase cost.	☑		
• Issues are valued at the average of the cost of purchases.			☑
• Inventory is valued at the most recent purchase cost.	☑		
• Inventory is valued at the oldest purchase cost.		☑	

Workbook Activity 10

Method	Cost of issue on 23 March	Closing stock at 31 March
FIFO	£750	£1,650
LIFO	£850	£1,550
AVCO	£787.50	£1,612.50

Workings

FIFO

- The issue will be made up of all 100 units from March 5, all 100 units from March 12 and 100 of those purchased on March 19 at a price of £600/200 = £3 per unit.

- Cost of issue = £200 + £250 + (100 × £3) = £750

- Total purchases = £200 + £250 + £600 + £1,350 = £2,400

- Closing stock = £2,400 – £750 = £1,650

LIFO

- The issue will be made up of all 200 units from March 19 and 100 units from March 12 at a price of £250/100 = £2.50 per unit.

- Cost of issue = £600 + (100 × £2.50) = £850

- Closing stock = £2,400 − £850 = £1,550

AVCO

- Before March 23 we had bought a total of 400 units at a total cost of 200 + 250 + 600 = £1,050

- On average this works out at £1,050/400 = £2.625 per unit

- Thus the cost of the issue will be 300 × £2.625 = £787.50

- Closing stock = £2,400 − £787.5 = £1,612.50

 Workbook Activity 11

Identify the following statements as either true or false.

Statement	True	False
• FIFO costs issues of stock at the oldest purchase price.	☑	
• AVCO values closing stock at the oldest purchase price.		☑
• LIFO costs issues of stock at the oldest purchase price.		☑

Workbook Activity 12

Element	Total cost	Unit cost
Materials	£200,000	£10.00
Labour	£100,000	£5.00
Overheads	£150,000	£7.50
Total	£450,000	£22.50

Workbook Activity 13

Units	Fixed costs	Variable costs	Total costs	Unit cost
1,000	£200,000	£5,000	£205,000	£205.00
2,000	£200,000	£10,000	£210,000	£105.00
3,000	£200,000	£15,000	£215,000	£71.67
4,000	£200,000	£20,000	£220,000	£55.00

Workbook Activity 14

	£
Opening inventory of raw materials	2,800
Purchases of raw materials	12,000
Closing inventory of raw materials	(2,000)
DIRECT MATERIALS USED	12,800
Direct labour	7,200
DIRECT COST	**20,000**
Manufacturing overheads	9,400
MANUFACTURING COST	**29,400**
Opening inventory of work in progress	8,400
Closing inventory of work in progress	(6,400)
COST OF GOODS MANUFACTURED	**31,400**
Opening inventory of finished goods	12,000
Closing inventory of finished goods	(14,000)
COST OF GOODS SOLD	**29,400**

4 Labour costs

Workbook Activity 8

Worker	Hours worked	Basic wage £	Overtime £	Gross wage £
M. Khan	42	370	75	445
D. Murphy	37	370	0	370
K. Ng	40	370	45	415

Workbook Activity 9

Worker	Units produced in week	Gross wage £
H. Potter	100 units	250.00
T. Riddle	130 units	325.00
S. Snape	175 units	437.50

Workbook Activity 10

Day	Units produced	Gross wage £
Monday	4 units	25
Tuesday	6 units	30
Wednesday	9 units	45
Thursday	3 units	25
Friday	8 units	40
Total	30 units	165

Workbook Activity 11

Worker	Hours worked	Units produced	Basic wage £	Bonus £	Gross wage £
L. Aragon	37	375	444	5	449
T. Ent	35	360	420	10	430
K. Theodin	42	410	504	0	504

5 Budgeting

Workbook Activity 7

Cost type	Budget £	Actual £	Variance £	Adv.	Fav.
Sales	175,000	176,850	1,850		☑
Labour	15,000	14,950	50		☑
Overheads	120,600	120,000	600		☑

Workbook Activity 8

Statement	True	False
A variance is the difference between actual and budgeted cost.	☑	
A variance is the average of actual and budgeted cost.		☑
A favourable variance means this cost element would reduce profit compared to budget.		☑
An adverse variance means you have made a saving compared to budgeted costs.		☑

Workbook Activity 9

Cost type	Budget	Actual	Variance	Significant?	
	£	£	£	Yes	No
Direct labour	10,000	9,500	500		☑
Direct materials	13,000	15,200	2,200	☑	
Production overheads	24,000	25,120	1,120		☑
Administration costs	35,000	32,400	2,600	☑	
Selling and distribution costs	45,000	49,260	4,260	☑	

6 Spreadsheets

Workbook Activity 7

Statement	True	False
Spreadsheets will not allow data entered into the cells to be rearranged.		☑
If a password is used, it must also be the title of the spreadsheet.		☑
A formula tells the spreadsheet to undertake a particular action or calculation.	☑	
Worksheets refer to the different pages of the spreadsheet.	☑	

Workbook Activity 8

The figures need to be placed into descending order (Z to A) – so the figures need to run from the highest to the lowest.

This would give us:

B
Wages (£)
201
195
177
176

Cell B3 therefore contains 195– which gives us answer D.

Workbook Activity 9

(a)

	A	B	C	D	E	F
1		**Budget**	**Actual**	**Variance**	**Adv or Fav**	**Significant (S) or Not significant (NS)**
2	**Sales**	1,500	1,670	170	F	S
3	**Materials**	895	997	102	A	S
4	**Labour**	450	403	47	F	S
5	**Overheads**	315	295	20	F	NS

(b)   The most appropriate formulas would have been:

	D
1	**Variance**
2	=B2-C2
3	=B3-C3
4	=B4-C4
5	=B5-C5

MOCK ASSESSMENT

1 Mock Assessment Questions

Task 1

Costing uses a number of techniques to assist management.

(a) Identify the following statements as being true or false by putting a tick in the relevant column of the table below.

Statement	True	False
• The piecework method can be used to cost issues and value inventory.		
• FIFO is a useful inventory valuation method for perishable goods.		
• A variance is always adverse if the actual figure is greater than the budget.		
• Classification of cost by function is especially useful if preparing financial statements.		

The table below lists some characteristics of financial accounting and management accounting.

(b) Indicate the characteristics for each system by putting a tick in the relevant column of the table below.

Characteristic	Financial accounting	Management accounting
• This system is designed to aid control and planning for the organisation.		
• This system produces information that will be primarily used by internal stakeholders.		
• This system will produce a statement of financial position.		
• This system calculates the cost of the products that the organisation makes.		

Task 2

Pet Care Ltd is a veterinary practice.

(a) **Classify the following costs by element (material, labour or overhead) by putting a tick in the relevant column of the table below.**

Cost	Material	Labour	Overhead
• Antiseptic lotion used on injuries.			
• Wages of veterinarian.			
• Bandages.			
• Insurance of premises.			

(b) **Classify the following costs incurred by nature (direct or indirect) by putting a tick in the relevant column of the table below.**

Cost	Direct	Indirect
• Cleaning materials for the practice.		
• Wages of the receptionist.		
• Rent of the practice buildings.		
• Medicines given to animals.		

Task 3

Pear plc manufactures computers.

(a) **Classify the following costs incurred by function (production, administration, selling and distribution or finance) by putting a tick in the relevant column of the table below.**

Cost	Production	Admin	Selling and Distribution	Finance
• Glass for making computer screens.				
• Depreciation of delivery vans.				
• Insurance for office buildings.				
• Bank charges.				

(b) **Classify the following costs by their behaviour (fixed, variable or semi-variable) by putting a tick in the relevant column of the table below.**

Cost	Fixed	Variable	Semi-variable
• Annual salary of Pear's directors.			
• Car hire consisting of an annual fee plus a usage charge.			
• Purchase of metal used in the manufacture of computers.			
• Wages of factory staff, who are paid on a piecework basis.			

Task 4

Pet Care Ltd operates a veterinary practice and uses a coding system for its elements of cost (materials, labour or overheads) and then further classifies each element by nature (direct or indirect cost) as below. So, for example, the code for direct materials is A100.

Element of cost	Code	Nature of cost	Code
Materials	A	Direct	100
		Indirect	200
Labour	B	Direct	100
		Indirect	200
Overheads	C	Direct	100
		Indirect	200

Code the following costs, extracted from invoices and payroll, using the table below.

Cost	Code
• Stationary materials used by receptionist.	
• Medicines prescribed to pets.	
• Salary of veterinary nurse.	
• Legal costs to negotiate lease of new premises.	
• Wages of receptionist.	

Task 5

Mombok Ltd, a computer manufacturer, uses a numerical coding structure based on one profit centre and three cost centres as outlined below. Each code has a sub-code so each transaction will be coded as ***/***

Profit/Cost centre	Code	Sub-classification	Sub-code
Sales	100	European sales	100
		US sales	200
Production	200	Direct cost	100
		Indirect cost	200
Administration	300	Direct cost	100
		Indirect cost	200
Selling and Distribution	400	Direct cost	100
		Indirect cost	200

Code the following revenue and expense transactions, which have been extracted from purchase invoices, sales invoices and payroll, using the table below.

Transaction	Code
Accounts department salaries.	
Packing boxes for computers.	
Sales to France, Europe.	
Package and posting costs to individual customers.	
Graphics cards for computers.	
Factory canteen wages.	

Task 6

(a) **Identify the type of cost behaviour (fixed, variable or semi-variable) described in each statement by putting a tick in the relevant column of the table below.**

Cost	Fixed	Variable	Semi-variable
• Costs of £15,000 are made up of a fixed element of £10,000 as well as a £5 per unit charge on the 1,000 units made.			
• Total cost per unit is £4 when 1,000 units are made, or £8 when 500 units are made.			
• Costs are £15,000 at 5,000 units and £9,000 at 3,000 units.			

(b) **Classify the following costs as either fixed or variable by putting a tick in the relevant column of the table below.**

Costs	Fixed	Variable
• Annual audit of the business.		
• Wages paid to employees on a piecework system with a bonus per unit if they produce more than a set number of units.		
• Cost of petrol for a delivery company.		

Task 7

(a) **Indicate whether the following costs are an overhead or not by putting a tick in the relevant column of the table below.**

Cost	Yes	No
Fee paid for an annual health and safety inspection.		
Stationery provided to all departments within the organisation.		
Materials used to manufacture the product.		

Joiner Ltd makes a single product. At a production level of 55,000 units it has the following costs:

Materials	110,000 kilos at £44 per kilo
Labour	10,000 hours at £18 per hour
Overheads	£4,070,000

(b) **Complete the table below to show the unit product cost at the production level of 55,000 units.**

Element	Unit cost
Materials	
Labour	
Direct cost	
Overheads	
Total	

Task 8

(a) Reorder the following costs into a manufacturing account format for the year ended 31 December. Use the columns to the right of the table below to enter your answer.

Purchases of raw materials	25,000		
Direct labour	45,000		
Opening inventory of finished goods	35,000		
COST OF GOODS SOLD			
Opening inventory of raw materials	6,000		
DIRECT MATERIALS USED			
Manufacturing overheads	87,000		
Opening inventory of work in progress	12,000		
Closing inventory of finished goods	14,000		
MANUFACTURING COST			
Closing inventory of work in progress	14,000		
Closing inventory of raw materials	16,000		
DIRECT COST			
COST OF GOODS MANUFACTURED			

Task 8, continued

(b) Enter the correct figures for the following costs which were not provided in part (a)

DIRECT MATERIALS USED	£	
DIRECT COST	£	
MANUFACTURING COST	£	
COST OF GOODS MANUFACTURED	£	
COST OF GOODS SOLD	£	

Task 9

Fisk Ltd carries a single type of raw material. At the start of the month, there were 2,500 kilos of the material in inventory, valued at £8 per kilo. During the month, Fisk bought another 5,000 kilos of material for £7.25 per kilo. The following week he issues 6,000 kilos to production.

(a) Identify the valuation method described in the statements below by putting a tick in the relevant column.

Statement	FIFO	LIFO	AVCO
The closing inventory is valued at £12,000.			
The issue of 6,000 units is costed at £45,000.			
The issue of 6,000 units is costed at £45,375.			

(b) Identify whether the statements in the table below are true or false by putting a tick in the relevant column.

Statement	True	False
FIFO values closing inventory at £11,250.		
AVCO values closing inventory at £10,875.		
LIFO costs the issue of 6,000 units at £44,250.		

Task 10

Tiphook Ltd has the following movements in a certain type of inventory into and out of its stores for the month of April:

DATE	RECEIPTS		ISSUES	
	Units	Cost	Units	Cost
April 1	150	£900		
April 15	400	£2,600		
April 22	350	£2,800		
April 27			500	
April 30	200	£1,300		

Complete the table below for the issue and closing inventory values.

Method	Cost of issue on 27 April	Closing inventory at 30 April
FIFO	£	£
LIFO	£	£
AVCO	£	£

Task 11

An employee is paid £7.50 per hour and is expected to make 45 units per hour. Any excess production will be paid a bonus of £0.75 per unit.

(a) **Identify the following statements as being true or false by putting a tick in the relevant column of the table below.**

Statement	True	False
During a 28 hour working week, if the employee produces 1,265 units they would not receive a bonus.		
During a 32 hour working week, if the employee produces 1,485 units they will receive a £33.75 bonus.		
During a 45 hour working week, if the employee produces 2,100 units they will receive total pay of £395.75		

Magic Ltd pays a time-rate of £8 per hour to its direct labour for a standard 38 hour week. Any of the labour force working in excess of 38 hours is paid an overtime rate of £12 per hour.

(b) **Calculate the basic wage, overtime and gross wage for the week for the two employees in the table below. Note: if no overtime is paid, you should enter 0 as the overtime for that employee.**

Worker	Hours worked	Basic wage	Overtime	Gross wage
D Mooney	38			
A Bhardwa	43			

Task 12

Identify the following statements regarding labour payment methods as either true or false by putting a tick in the relevant column of the table below.

Statement	True	False
Piecework systems encourage staff to improve the quality of their work.		
The overtime premium refers to the amount over and above the normal hourly rate that employees are paid for overtime hours.		
Time related pay systems reward staff for being more productive.		
Piecework systems give an assured level of remuneration to employees.		

Task 13

Hurricane Ltd uses a time-rate method with overtime to pay its employees. It pays its staff £5.50 per hour for a standard 34 hour week. Any hours above this are paid at double time.

Calculate the basic wage, overtime and gross pay for the week for the three employees in the table below. Note: if no overtime is paid, you should enter 0 as the bonus for that employee in the table.

Worker	Hours worked	Basic wage £	Overtime £	Gross wage £
S. Torm	38			
T. Ornado	32			
T. Wister	44			

Task 14

Jericho plc has started the production of a spreadsheet that will enable it to calculate its profit for each week of the previous month. There were no opening or closing inventories.

Jericho had the following information for the four weeks in the last month:

Units sold: Week 1 – 2,000

Week 2 – 2,400

Week 3 – 2,100

Week 4 – 1,700

Variable costs £4.50 per unit

Sales £6.50 per unit

Fixed costs £1,600 per week

	A	B	C	D	E	F
1		Fixed costs £	?	?	Sales	?
2	Week 1	1,600	9,000	10,600	13,000	2,400
3	Week 2					
4	Week 3					
5	Week 4					
6	Total					

(a) **Decide which of the following headings should be entered into each of the cells C1, D1 and F1.**

Variable costs

Profit/(loss)

Total costs

Cell	Heading
C1	
D1	
E1	

(b) Complete the table by entering the correct figures into the above table for rows 3 to 6 inclusive.

(c) Insert the formulas in the table below that you used for row 6 of columns B, C, D and F. (Note: column E is not required)

	A	B	C	D	F
6	Total				

Task 15

Listed below are some statements about spreadsheets.

Identify the statements as being true or false by putting a tick in the relevant column.

Statement	True	False
Spreadsheets enable data to be presented in a number of different ways, such as lists and graphs.		
Data is entered into the active cell of a spreadsheet.		
Spreadsheets are open-source, meaning that there is no way to limit access to the information they contain.		
Data in the active cell will be shown both within the active cell itself as well as in the formula bar.		

Task 16

Passlow Ltd has produced a performance report detailing budgeted and actual cost for last month.

(a)   Calculate the amount of the variance for each cost type and enter it into the spreadsheet below. Determine whether the variance is adverse or favourable (enter A or F).

	A	B	C	D	E
1	Cost type	Budget £	Actual £	Variance	Adverse or favourable (A or F)
2	Sales revenue	125,000	126,100		
3	Direct materials	19,200	20,100		
4	Direct labour	36,800	36,400		
5	Overheads	33,000	36,000		

(b)   Insert the formulas in the table below that you used in cells 2, 3, 4 and 5 of <u>column D</u> of the spreadsheet.

	D
1	Variance
2	
3	
4	
5	

Task 17

Kyle Ltd has produced a performance report detailing budgeted and actual cost for last quarter. Any variance in excess of 5% of budget is deemed to be significant and should be reviewed.

(a) **In column E, identify significant variances in excess of 5% of budget, entering S for significant and NS for not significant.**

	A	B	C	D	E
1	Cost type	Budget £	Actual £	Variance	Significant (S) or Not significant (NS)
2	Direct materials	15,000	16,000	1,000	
3	Direct labour	42,000	44,000	2,000	
4	Production overheads	30,000	32,000	2,000	
5	Administration overheads	16,000	16,500	500	

Kyle wishes to sort the actual costs in column C into ascending order.

(b) **Place the figures from column C (cells C2 to C5 inclusive) in ascending order into the table below.**

	C
1	Actual £
2	
3	
4	
5	

2 Mock Assessment Answers

SECTION 1

Task 1(a)

- False
- True
- False*
- True

*Note that if actual sales were larger than budget sales, this would be a favourable variance.

Task 1(b)

- Management accounting
- Management accounting
- Financial accounting
- Management accounting

Task 2(a)

- Material
- Labour
- Material
- Overhead

Task 2(b)

- Indirect
- Indirect
- Indirect
- Direct

Task 3(a)

- Production
- Selling and distribution
- Administration
- Finance

Task 3(b)

- Fixed
- Semi-variable
- Variable
- Variable

Task 4

- A200
- A100
- B100
- C200
- B200

Task 5

- 300/200
- 400/100
- 100/100
- 400/100
- 200/100
- 200/200

Task 6(a)

- Semi-variable
- Fixed
- Variable

Task 6(b)

- Fixed
- Variable
- Variable

Task 7(a)

- Yes
- Yes
- No

Task 7(b)

Element	Unit cost
Materials	88
Labour	99
Direct costs	187
Overheads	74
Total	261

Task 8 (a)

Opening inventory of raw materials	6,000
Purchases of raw materials	25,000
Closing inventory of raw materials	16,000
DIRECT MATERIALS USED	
Direct labour	45,000
DIRECT COST	
Manufacturing overheads	87,000
MANUFACTURING COST	
Opening inventory of work in progress	12,000
Closing inventory of work in progress	14,000
COST OF GOODS MANUFACTURED	
Opening inventory of finished goods	35,000
Closing inventory of finished goods	14,000
COST OF GOODS SOLD	

Task 8(b)

DIRECT MATERIALS USED	£	15,000
DIRECT COST	£	60,000
MANUFACTURING COST	£	147,000
COST OF GOODS MANUFACTURED	£	145,000
COST OF SALES	£	166,000

Task 9(a)

- LIFO
- AVCO
- FIFO

Task 9(b)

- False
- False
- True

Task 10

Method	Issue cost	Closing stock
FIFO	£3,175	£4,425
LIFO	£3,775	£3,825
AVCO	£3,500	£4,100

Task 11(a)

- False
- True
- False

Task 11(b)

Worker	Hours worked	Basic wage	Overtime	Gross wage
D Mooney	38	£304	£0	£304
A Bhardwa	43	£304	£60	£364

Task 12

- False
- True
- False
- False

Task 13

Worker	Hours worked	Basic wage £	Overtime £	Gross wage £
S. Torm	38	187	44	231
T. Ornado	32	176	0	176
T. Wister	44	187	110	297

Task 14 (a)

Cell	Heading
C1	Variable costs
D1	Total costs
E1	Profit/(loss)

Task 14 (b)

	A	B	C	D	E	F
1		Fixed costs £	?	?	Sales	?
2	Week 1	1,600	9,000	10,600	13,000	2,400
3	Week 2	1,600	10,800	12,400	15,600	3,200
4	Week 3	1,600	9,450	11,050	13,650	2,600
5	Week 4	1,600	7,650	9,250	11,050	1,800
6	Total	6,400	36,900	43,300	53,300	10,000

Task 14(c)

	A	B	C	D	E	F
6	Total	=sum(B2:B5)	=sum(C2:C5)	=sum(D2:D5)		=sum(F2:F5)

Note that other answers would have also been acceptable, for instance:

	A	B	C	D	F
6	Total	=B2+B3+B4 +B5	=C2+C3+C4 +C5	=D2+D3+D4 +D5	=F2+F3+F4 +F5

The total for F6 could also have been found by using the formula: =E6-D6

Task 15

- True
- True
- False
- True

Task 16(a)

	A	B	C	D	E
1	Cost type	Budget £	Actual £	Variance	Adverse or favourable (A or F)
2	Sales revenue	125,000	126,100	1,100	F
3	Direct materials	19,200	20,100	900	A
4	Direct labour	36,800	36,400	400	F
5	Overheads	33,000	36,000	3,000	A

Task 16(b)

	D
1	Variance
2	=B2-C2
3	=B3-C3
4	=B4-C4
5	=B5-C5

Task 17(a)

	A	B	C	D	E
1	Cost type	Budget £	Actual £	Variance	Significant (S) or Not significant (NS)
2	Direct materials	15,000	16,000	1,000	**S**
3	Direct labour	42,000	44,000	2,000	**NS**
4	Production overheads	30,000	32,000	2,000	**S**
5	Administration overheads	16,000	16,500	500	**NS**

Task 17(b)

	C
1	Actual £
2	16,000
3	16,500
4	32,000
5	44,000

INDEX

A

Administrative costs, 7

Adverse variance, 93

Aims of management accounting, 3

Authorisation, 89

B

Bin cards, 60

Bonus schemes, 77

Budgetary control, 88, 104

Budgeting, 88, 104, 121

C

Calculating a cost per unit, 51

Calculating gross pay, 72

Coding
  in practice, 30
  problems, 33
  systems, 24

Communicating, 3

Communication and co-ordination, 89

Control, 4

Controlling, 3

Co-ordinating, 3

Cost
  accounting, 4
  centre(s), 5, 6
  codes, 24
  coding, 24
  sales, 7

Cost classification, 6
  by behaviour, 10
  by element, 8
  by function, 7
  by nature, 9

D

Decision making, 4

Different types of stock, 40

Direct and indirect labour, 72

Direct costs, 9

Distribution costs, 7

E

Evaluating the significance of a variance,
  95, 117, 118

Evaluation, 89

F

Factory cost of goods sold, 54

Favourable variance, 93

FIFO (first in, first out), 42

Financial accounting, 2

Finished goods, 41

Fixed costs, 10

Forecasting, 89

H

Hourly rate employees, 73

I

Indirect costs, 9

Investment centre, 6

L

Labour, 8
  costs, 72

LIFO (last in, first out), 42

M

Management accounting, 2

Management information, 3

Materials, 8, 40
  purchasing cycle, 56

Motivating, 3

Motivation, 89

O

Output related pay, 75

Overheads, 8

Overtime, 74

P

Payment by results, 76

Piece rate with guarantee, 76

Planning, 3, 4, 89

Production cycle, 40

Profit centre, 6

Purchase
  invoices, 59
  orders, 58

Purpose of cost codes, 29

R

Reasons for budgeting, 89, 105

S

Salaried employees, 73

Semi-variable costs, 11

Stepped costs, 11

Stores ledger account, 60

T

Time related pay, 73

V

Valuing raw materials, 42

Valuing WIP and finished goods, 49

Variable costs, 10

Variances, 93, 114

W

Weighed average (AVCO), 42

Work in progress, 41

KAPLAN PUBLISHING